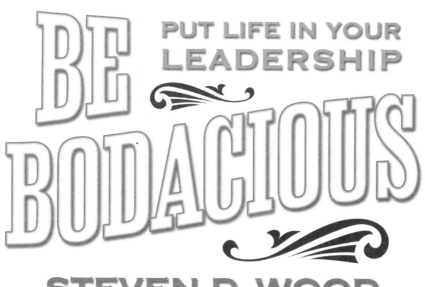

PUT LIFE IN YOUR LEADERSHIP

BE BODACIOUS

STEVEN D. WOOD

WHITE BAY PUBLISHING • ALLEN, TEXAS

BE BODACIOUS
Put Life in Your Leadership

www.Be-Bodacious.com

© 2010 Steven D. Wood

Published by:

SAN: >>>>>>>>   859-5038   <<<<<<<<<<<

WHITE BAY PUBLISHING
101C North Greenville Avenue #249
Allen, Texas 75002

Cover and interior design by TLC Graphics, *www.TLCGraphics.com*
Cover: Monica Thomas; *Interior:* Erin Stark
Back cover author photo by: Larry Fleming Photography

Printed in the U.S.A.

ISBN: 978-0-9844777-0-8

Library of Congress Control Number: 2010923542

THIS BOOK IS DEDICATED TO KAY, MY HIGH SCHOOL sweetheart, best friend and wife. Her support over the years has been my source of motivation and inspiration to "Be Bodacious and Put Life in My Leadership." Also, I dedicate this book to my father and my mentors who imparted their wisdom and modeled integrity in their lives and leadership. To my children and grand-children who bring continued joy in my life.

Table of Contents

Section III: The Bodacious Secrets Passed On

Introduction

BODACIOUS LEADERSHIP GOES BEYOND JOB TITLE OR position and requires leadership in both your professional and personal life. Bodacious Leadership begins with an extraordinary commitment to your dream, unrestrained passion toward pursuing your dream, and bold action to realize your dream.

If you enjoy inspiring stories of accomplishment and are eager to know how you can "Put Life in Your Leadership", then you selected the right book. This book tells the story of Josh, a young man unsatisfied with the ordinary. In his search, he discovers the secrets of success from a journal given to him by his mentor, simply known as Cowboy. In his journal, Cowboy shares his adventures and the leaders who influenced him, allowing him to discover the Bodacious Leadership Secrets.

The stories shared in this book will make you laugh and maybe even make you cry, but more importantly, they will move you to action. This is not a typical "how to" leadership book. Instead, entertaining stories are used to illustrate life-changing secrets and to reveal the benefits of being an extraordinary, unrestrained, and bold leader.

Cowboy is truly the Bodacious Leader. He is the embodiment of all the effective leaders who affected this author's life and leadership.

I hope you enjoy the motivating and humorous stories in this book and discover how you, too, can be an extraordinary, unrestrained, and bold leader, one who pursues bodacious opportunities, gives more to others, grows from adversity, and enjoys an adventurous life.

SECTION I

Josh Meets Cowboy

CHAPTER ONE

Pursuing the Bodacious Secrets

JOSH LOOKED AT HIS BABY GIRL AND WIFE across the breakfast table. He was proud to be a husband and new father. What could be better? After all, he had married his high school sweetheart, had a beautiful baby girl and a roof over his head. Josh, eighteen–years-old, and his seventeen-years-old wife, Sarah, were not bothered that "the roof over their head" was a twelve-foot by sixty-foot yellow and white trailer. The little trailer with harvest gold shag carpet and walls so thin if you got a running start you could easily run through them was home. Sure, they hoped to have a house without wheels, but that seemed so far in the future and beyond their budget that it was no more than a dream.

People in the trailer park were nice to the young couple and went out of their way to help. Everyone but Josh and Sarah could see that they were "poor," but when you are eighteen years old, things seemed much simpler. Money was in short supply, but time appeared endless and love blinded them to the reality of their situation. Josh and Sarah never thought in terms of being "poor," they just knew there was only so much money to spend, and when it was gone, there was no more. Luxuries such as getting a hamburger at Dairy Queen were beyond their means. Instead, fried bologna supreme, a gourmet dish to them, was a regular weekend treat. In a strange sort of way, lack of possessions and money provided fertile soil for this young naïve couple to grow their love and commitment to one another. Theirs was not a textbook beginning to a marriage. To both of them, it was as if they were writing chapter one of a new book, and they still had hundreds of unwritten chapters to fill with new adventures.

Even with all his optimism, Josh felt in his soul that there was more out there to be discovered. Deep inside there was a dream of going to undiscovered places, meeting new people, landing a high paying job or even moving away from the small Texas town where he was raised. He was not sure what fanned this small distant flame in his soul, but it simmered, waiting to leap out and catapult him beyond his imagination. Each day there was the reality of making a living and coming home to his two beautiful girls at night. But his dreams persisted.

Josh's brother-in-law, Alan helped Josh secure a good steady job where he was working. Josh's job at the factory was working on the loading dock. The work was hard and it was awful hot in the summer, but Josh was glad to have the work and was thankful to Alan for his help. Josh grew up working on a farm and was used to hard physical activity and working outdoors. Working on the loading dock, while not outdoors, allowed him to be active and do different things. After being on the loading dock for a while his boss offered him the opportunity to "move up" to one of the assembly lines. He gladly accepted the new position and was proud of himself for being offered a promotion so quickly. Josh had never worked on an assembly line and had no idea what he would do on the new job. There were hundreds of people working on the assembly line. Some of them had been there for decades, which lead Josh to believe it must be a good job. Why else would people stay there for so many years? Josh's new job was to put a piece of sheet metal into a machine that would form it to a finished part. All day long he put a piece of sheet metal into the machine that produced hundreds of finished parts.

During the long days, he would avoid looking at the large clock that hung like a taskmaster over the assembly line. The clock determined when work started, when you went to the bathroom, and when your day ended. The huge taskmaster moved slowly and at times seemed to move in reverse. Working on an assembly line controlled by the taskmaster clock, doing the same thing repeatedly was confining, monotonous work for Josh. After a couple of weeks working on the assembly line, he asked to go back to his old job on the loading dock. His boss advised Josh he was passing up a good opportunity, as working on the assembly line was considered the best job in the factory. Josh persisted and thankfully, his boss moved him back to the loading dock where he had freedom of movement and freedom from the taskmaster clock. But even on the loading dock, Josh felt he needed something more in life. He wanted an education.

Josh attended community college at night with the hope of someday receiving a college diploma. In a prideful sort of way, he thought it would feel good to be the first in his family to receive a college degree. Josh wasn't completely certain what he could do with a college diploma or what doors it might open, but pride continued to be a good motivator. Growing up in a small town did not expose young people to many professions beyond blue-collar jobs, so Josh was ignorant of professional job possibilities beyond farm or factory work. Deep down though, he knew there was more to learn and more to life than spending forty years at the same factory, working for the taskmaster clock, or on a loading dock.

Josh liked his job on the loading dock, but he often day-dreamed about working in the front office. Wearing a necktie to work or having an office was a big dream for a dockworker. Josh did not talk to anyone other than Sarah about his big dream. In a small blue-collar town, crossing over to a "big wig" job was considered taboo, something that folks from a small town just did not do. Sarah supported Josh in his big dream and gave him, loving encouragement to continue his pursuit.

The dream buried deep inside him came to life every morning when the owner of the company, affectingly known by the workers as "Cowboy," walked through the warehouse, greeting workers on the loading dock. Josh was amazed that the owner of the company seemed like such a regular person. It made him feel good when Cowboy called him by name and greeted him each morning. Josh vowed that if by a miracle he ever made it to the top, like Cowboy, that he would treat his employees the same way. Josh often wondered how Cowboy came to own a large company like this. He assumed that Cowboy probably came from a wealthy family and attended the best colleges. Surely, Cowboy had the advantage of wealth, a predestination reserved for the selected few.

Josh wanted to talk to Cowboy and find out more about how he became the owner. However, he could not get beyond, "Good morning, sir," when responding to Cowboy's greeting every morning. Cowboy was different from most people in his position; he seemed genuine, approachable, and like one of the "regular" people. Josh wondered if it was possible to approach Cowboy and ask him about his secrets of success.

Josh was a morning person, talkative and energized. Sarah was Josh's opposite, still every morning she prepared breakfast for Josh and listened as he talked about his dreams and plans for the day. One particular morning she was surprised to hear Josh tell her that he was going to ask Cowboy to spend time with him and share his secrets of success. Sarah thought that it was the coffee talking, but in her ever-encouraging way, she supported Josh's plans.

Josh went on to explain that Cowboy was different and that he took the time to walk the factory every morning and talk to the workers. For some unexplained reason, Josh believed that Cowboy would take the time to talk to him. Today was the day he would ask Cowboy to tell him about his secrets of success.

On his way to work that morning Josh rehearsed what he would say to Cowboy. Carefully playing out the event in his mind helped Josh subdue his anxiety about the encounter. The closer Josh got to the factory, the more he began to doubt what he was about to do and started to rationalize why he should back out. After all, he had a great job and could probably work at the factory for a long time. Why would he jeopardize his job for this high-risk encounter? After parking his car and turning off the engine, he began his walk to the factory door. Along the way, his fear abated and the adrenalin transformed to bold courage and excitement. As he walked through the factory door, Josh became convinced that Cowboy would talk to him.

Cowboy was surprised by Josh's request to meet with him. For years, he had walked the factory floor greeting the workers. Not once had anyone ever approached him and requested a meeting. Cowboy stood there for a few seconds and said nothing to Josh's request. Judging from the expression on Cowboy's face Josh assumed he made a mistake. As Josh begin to gaze down at the factory floor, Cowboy in his finest Texas drawl replied, "Son, I would like nothing better than to spend time with you, come to my office at 10:30 this morning and let's talk."

CHAPTER TWO

Bodacious Secrets Revealed

Josh was surprised that his co-workers gave him a hard time about asking Cowboy to meet with him. They cautioned Josh not to reveal too much about the day-to-day activities on the loading dock. His fellow workers theorized Cowboy was planning to take advantage of Josh's naivety to find out about what "really went on" in the factory. They went on to advise Josh that Cowboy might be setting him up. Josh, in his own stubborn way, felt proud and refused to go along with their scare tactics and remained resolute in his convictions that Cowboy would share something special with him.

Something about Cowboy gave Josh confidence and courage to continue forward, no matter what his co-workers told him. Josh was disappointed that his co-workers did not share his excitement or congratulate him about having an appointment with Cowboy. It seemed strange to Josh that they reacted in such a negative way and he supposed that maybe they were envious.

Although his co-workers did not support him or celebrate with him, Josh could hardly wait until the meeting. At 10:15 a.m. Josh began his journey to the front office for his meeting with Cowboy. Josh was excited and scared at the same time as he made the long walk through the factory to the front office. He had never been in the front office of the factory and tried to envision how it looked. He was concerned because he was in work clothes and thought he would be out of place in the office where everyone was certain to be dressed in nice clothes. Josh wondered if he could get past the front door, *What if Cowboy forgot to tell the receptionist that it is okay to let me in?* He did not know how he'd convince the receptionist that Cowboy had agreed to meet with him. Worse, he did not know what he would tell his co-workers if he did not get past the front door of the office. To his relief, a pleasant woman sitting behind a desk near the door met Josh when he entered the front office. When Josh told her about his meeting with Cowboy, she said with a smile, "He's expecting you, come with me and I will take you to his office."

Josh was impressed by how clean and organized everything was. The office environment was so different from the hot factory and loading dock. The sounds of forklift engines and factory machinery did not exist. The office was cool and comfortable. This was the environment Josh wanted to work in some day.

Weaving their way through the corridors of offices and cubicles, Josh followed his guide through a set of ornate wooden double doors that opened into Cowboys' large corner office. Windows that reached from the floor to ceilings wrapped around two sides of the office and overlooked a peaceful pond with a small park on the far shore. A large wooden desk sat well positioned near the windows to take advantage of the view of the lake. Two large chairs sat strategically in front of the desk to accommodate visitors. One entire wall of the office was consumed floor to ceiling by a huge bookcase stuffed with hundreds of books. On the walls of the office were numerous plaques and certificates of recognition. A certificate signed by the governor of Texas recognized outstanding volunteer service and another recognized dedicated service and contribution to his church. Hanging next to the certificates was a picture of a sailing yacht anchored in a palm-fringed bay surrounded by a sugar white beach. A small table was centered against the far wall. An old Bible with a tattered well-worn cover and stuffed with handwritten notes sat on the table.

On the wall directly above the table, was a picture of five rugged looking young cowboys posed together in front of an old barn. The faded picture of the cowboys stood out from all the other plaques and certificates. Looking closer at the cowboys in the picture, Josh wondered why this particular picture was hanging next to plaques and certificates of accomplishment. The old Bible and faded picture of five cowboys displayed so prominently among the other awards spurred Josh's curiosity.

"Wondering about that old picture and the Bible?" Cowboy asked Josh as he entered the office. Josh fixated on the picture, was unaware Cowboy had entered the office and was startled by the unexpected question.

"Have a seat and I'll tell you more about that picture." Cowboy sat down in the large chair behind his desk and motioned for Josh to take one of the chairs across from him.

Josh took his place in the large comfortable chair in front of Cowboy's desk. Once Josh settled, Cowboy asked, "Notice anything special about that picture of the five cowboys."

Josh studied the picture from his chair, looking for something obvious. Josh confessed, "Well it seems a bit out of place among the other plaques and awards."

Cowboy grinned. He stood, walked over to the wall, and took down the picture. He handed it to Josh and encouraged him to take a closer look. Then he returned to his chair behind the desk. Josh felt pressured to find something unusual about the picture. His session with Cowboy had not started the way he envisioned and Josh wondered where Cowboy was going.

"Good leaders have the ability to see things in people that others may not see," Cowboy told Josh. Look closely at the cowboy standing on the right wearing a blue shirt. "Do you see anything special about him?"

Josh tried to see what Cowboy wanted him to see. After what seemed to be an eternity Cowboy broke the silence, "Josh all you see is five rough looking Cowboys."

Josh nodded and handed the picture across the desk. Taking the picture in his hand, Cowboy pointed to the cowboy in the blue shirt and said, "You see a cowboy in the picture, but I see a business owner. Look closer, can you see him?"

Josh focused in on the cowboy's face. Although his large brimmed hat shadowed part of his face, making it difficult to make out the details, Josh did notice the young man in the blue shirt had facial features similar to the much older Cowboy sitting behind the big desk.

"Is that you in the picture?" Josh asked, pointing at the cowboy in the blue shirt.

"You seem wary. Why are you surprised that it might be me in the picture?" Cowboy asked.

Josh thought carefully on how he should reply to Cowboy's question. It seemed incomprehensible to him that someone who owned a large corporation would come from such a rough background. *Surely, Cowboy has educational credentials equal to or better than those on his staff,* Josh thought. After all, everyone on the factory floor and on the loading dock knew the guys in the "white shirts," namely those in the offices, on the sales staff, and in the field all had degrees from well known universities and colleges. The rough young cowboy in the picture did not fit the template in Josh's mind of a business leader.

Cowboy leaned back in his chair and smiled. He said, "Josh you're squirming like a worm on a fish hook, so I'll help you out. That is me in the picture when I was attending Cowboy University. Cowboy went on to explain that it was during his ranch hand days that he learned key principles. Principles that changed his life and helped shape him into who he was today.

"It's all right here," Cowboy said. He lay the picture face down on his desk, took off the back, and removed the photograph from the frame. He handed it back over to Josh. Josh took the picture, turned it over and read the hand written list:

BODACIOUS SECRETS
Be Extraordinary
Be Unrestrained
Be Bold

Cowboy saw the puzzled expression on Josh's face. "Written right there in front of you are the secrets that you asked me to share with you. If you choose to be extraordinary, unrestrained, and bold in everything you do, you will achieve more than you thought possible."

They're just six words, Josh thought. But he looked up and asked Cowboy, "Will you help me understand more about how I can be extraordinary, unrestrained, and bold? What do you mean by Bodacious Secrets?"

Cowboy opened a drawer on the side of his desk and removed an overstuffed brown envelop with CONFIDENTIAL written boldly across the front. Cowboy handed the envelope to Josh. "Go ahead, open the envelope, and look inside. All the secrets are in there. Everything you need to know to be extraordinary, unrestrained, and bold."

Josh lifted the metal clasps and unsealed the flap to open the envelope. He reached inside and removed a thick, well-worn leather bound journal. As Josh opened, the cover of the journal Cowboy began to explain, "Written on the pages of the journal you're holding is my personal collection of stories and notes that will help you understand Bodacious Secrets and how you can apply them to your life." Josh was amazed by Cowboy's generosity.

Cowboy leaned back in his chair and continued his story, "I started out working as a Cowboy for two outfits; one was a ranch on the Brazos River, and the other was a farm just outside the small town I was raised in. It was during those experiences as a cowboy that I learned important life principles, which I have carried with me through the years. However, there was a time that I did not live as close to the principles as I should have. Going from a Cowboy to owning a large company is a big step and a true blessing from God. In my case I did not always handle this unwarranted success as well as I should have. There were times I thought too highly of myself and became arrogant and prideful. I forgot about who I was, where I began, and who I wanted to become.

Rising from his chair, Cowboy walked across the room and stopped next to the table with the old Bible on it. "Prior to owning the company, I worked as part of the executive staff here. The pressure of expectations and performance started to weigh on me. It is funny how stress works on us. It sneaks up on us and before we know it, if we allow it to happen, stress will rob us of rational thinking and transform us into someone we do not want to be. That was exactly what happened to me and I did not even recognize it was happening. Looking back, I realize I was a real jerk at times because of my arrogance and pride. During this time I failed to embrace the secrets I learned when I was a cowboy. Early in my career, I remembered, "Where I came from" and embraced the principles. However, as I progressed up the company ladder, I found myself surrounded by some very good people who graduated from the finest universities with impressive professional pedigrees who intimidated me. Due to my competitive nature, I attempted to be as good as them. My problem was I focused on me and not the principles and the people who were responsible for my success."

Josh interrupted Cowboy, "Who are the people that were responsible for your success? Are you talking about the other cowboys in the picture?"

"Well, what I learned during my time as a cowboy played a part in my success, but there were other people along the way who had a big impact, too. In that journal are stories about people who influenced me throughout my life including my wife, family, my customers, and my work colleagues. None of us can find success alone. When I allowed myself to learn from others and leaned on others as a resource, the result was success.

"You do not have to be the smartest person in the organization; you just have to be the most bodacious person. You must have extraordinary commitment, take unrestrained action, and persist boldly. It is simple; if you surround yourself with extraordinary people, people who are the best in their field, then commit yourself to others such as your customers, you will have a bodacious combination.

The key to the Bodacious Secret is to gain support from people and customers of integrity who are accomplished at what they do. When I opened myself to this core principle, attracting extraordinary people and customers became easy. However, when I failed to live out the secrets and depended only on myself, stress and frustration followed.

"Prior to taking an executive position, I spent years working in the field. I had never worked in a large office or spent a lot of time going to meetings. My schedule was mine to set and I was free to prioritize my day to do things that I thought had the most impact. Then I got the opportunity to run a field office. I was the highest-level person out in the field. I set the culture and built a successful team of people who I trusted and was comfortable being around. Running a field operation was like running a ranch for an absent owner, who only showed up occasionally to check up on the operation. If things were going well, everyone pretty much left you alone and you ran your own operation. The field environment is an entrepreneurial environment where you are close to the action and close to the customer. Over the years, I had become proficient working in the field environment, and it was a good match for my style of leadership.

When I was offered an executive position, it meant relocating to the corporate office. My wife, Mattie, and I had a lot of discussion about the opportunity. It meant moving to another city far away from our grandchildren whom we enjoyed spending our time with. We spent a lot of time talking about how the promotion would impact family life. However, I didn't give much thought to the professional changes that would occur in the transition. I really underestimated the professional changes and challenges that were in store for me working in the corporate office. To make a long story short, I accepted the position and we began the process of relocation. Uprooting from where you live is never easy, but this relocation was particularly difficult. Leaving our family was tough, but we also had strong ties to our local community where we had many close friends.

Moving to the corporate office environment was new and uncomfortable for me. In the field, I had more control over my calendar and spent little time in meetings that I did not organize. In the corporate office I was no longer the highest-ranking person in the office, there were other people above me. Even though I had over two hundred employees in my organization, none of them worked in the corporate office; they all worked in the field offices.

It had been many years since I worked where my direct supervisor was so near to me and in daily contact to me.

Then there were so many meetings! I soon found my schedule consumed by meetings called by other people who seemed to have constant demands for my time. Not only were the meetings time hogs, they were ineffective and used of too many personnel resources. Meetings often included twenty people, when only half that number would have been enough. Too many people doing too little for too long, was the way I summed up most of the meetings. It amazed me how it would take two hours to cover thirty minutes of material in these meetings. There were times I felt like a professional meeting attendee instead of a leader of a large field organization.

A new job in an uncomfortable environment, combined with my competitive nature and my insecurities, led to me placing a lot of pressure on myself. The result was stress. It was during this stressful time of my career that Mattie got me something very special for my birthday. She went to great lengths to obtain a copy of the picture of my four cowboy friends and me. The picture was taken at the end of a long day of working cattle many years ago, and I had forgotten the picture was even taken. Even today, I cannot remember who took the picture, but I am glad they did.

Mattie was my girlfriend when I was a cowboy, and we had known each other for many years. She knew I needed to remember where I came from and that I needed to rediscover the secrets that helped me obtain higher levels of responsibility in the corporation. Looking at the picture brought back many good memories of working as a cowboy and of my friends. It also caused me to reflect on how far I had come from that dirty cattle pen to this comfortable corner office."

Cowboy moved across the office, sat in the chair next to Josh and continued to explain, "After Mattie gave me the picture I decided to write down the secrets that made a difference in my life and lead-

17

ership. I never again wanted to drift from the secrets that were core to my success. That evening, I stayed late in my office to reflect on my life and my career. As I sat there alone, I wrote down the Bodacious Secrets: be extraordinary, be unrestrained, and be bold on the back of the picture. That evening I began to journal about the people and events that helped me discover the bodacious secrets. I carry a copy of the picture with me and look at it often to remind me where I came from and to encourage me to live the secrets."

Cowboy paused a moment and then continued, "Josh, if you demonstrate extraordinary commitment, take unrestrained action, and are bold in getting things done; you can achieve great things.

When Cowboy stopped talking, Josh took the opportunity to ask, "Is this the reason everyone calls you Cowboy?"

Cowboy replied, "No. One of the guys I worked with gave me the nickname. He said I talked like a cowboy and the nickname just stuck. I really did not like it when everyone started calling me Cowboy. I was a little self-conscious about my Texas accent and felt people were making fun of me. However, after a while, I became comfortable with the nickname, and it kind of gave me a unique identity."

He walked over to the window and gazed out at the scene before him. "Actually I've never shared my story with anyone else other than Mattie and now you, Josh. Few people know my full background, and when they've asked about the cowboy picture on my office wall I tell them it's just a few old friends".

"Why did you decide to tell me your story?" asked Josh. "You barely know me. Other than the morning greetings as you walk through the warehouse each day, we've never spoke."

Cowboy explained, "I know more about you than you might think. Your boss has told me you are an honest, hard working young man with a wife and a new baby and that you have potential. You displayed extraordinary, unrestrained, and bold courage when you asked me to share with you how I became successful. From your actions, I saw a young man with a hunger to succeed. Someone who can live out the bodacious secrets and I believe that after you read the journal, you'll understand why I chose you."

Cowboy took the journal from Josh, placed it on his desk and in a stern voice, he asked, "Josh are you serious about understanding the bodacious secrets? Do you want to be an extraordinary, unrestrained and bold leader?"

Josh looked Cowboy straight in the eye and replied, "Thank you for telling me your story. Now that I have heard it, I am convinced more than ever that you can help me."

Flashing his signature grin, Cowboy replied, "Okay, I will share more with you. However, you are going to have to work and do this exactly as I instruct you. If you are willing to sacrifice and change, you can learn the principles. You must be willing to go far beyond learning them, you must commit to making them a part of your life and living them daily. It is one thing to know what to do; it is something all together different when you live out what you know."

THE CHALLENGE

"There are three things you must commit to doing every day. First, set aside an hour and a half for personal study time each day, Saturday and Sunday included. Second, read the secrets written on the back of the cowboy picture every day. In addition, read one chapter from the journal each day. Do this every day until you have read the entire journal. Finally, return both the picture and journal to me and we will talk again. Remember; set aside an hour and a half every day. Read the secrets, and read one chapter in the journal. Are you willing to do that?"

"Yes, sir, I will do it!" Josh responded exuberantly, "But are you telling me that you are going to give me your only copy of the journal and the picture?"

"No, I am giving you copies that you and you alone have my permission to read. The rest is up to you, Josh. If you want to know the secrets, and if you want to live an extraordinary, unrestrained, and bold life: here it is for you to learn. Now, it's time for you to get back and do an extraordinary job in the warehouse. Lock this envelope in your locker until you leave for home today."

Josh reached across the large desk for the envelope and with a crack in his voice replied. "Thank you, Cowboy. Thank you for taking the time to talk with me today. I want to be extraordinary, unrestrained, and bold in everything I do and I promise to get up early every day to read the secrets and the journal.

SECTION II

Cowboy's Journal

CHAPTER THREE

Take the Bodacious Ride

WHEN I WAS A YOUNG MAN WORKING AS A RANCH hand, we enjoyed going to the rodeos on the weekend. It was a lot of fun to watch my friend's rope, wrestle steers, and ride bucking horses and bulls. I was perfectly content to watch my friends and other people participate in the rodeo. While I did work on ranches, I never enjoyed riding a horse. So, rodeo events like roping and steer wrestling never appealed to me. The only thing that appealed to me less than riding and roping was riding a bucking horse or a bull. Horses are tall, and it is a long way to the ground when you fall off a bucking horse. All too often, the pain of the fall was complemented by a hard kick from the horse, delivered directly to the cowboy's body. While bulls are not as tall, they have a very foul disposition and love to get revenge by goring the cowboy with their horns or stomping the cowboy with their hooves. Each weekend I enjoyed hanging out at the rodeos, watching my

friends take on the horses, steers, and bulls, when my friends asked, "Why don't you ride a bull, are you chicken?"

I would always reply, "You guys are crazy if you think I am going to pay someone to let me get on a bull. I have better things to spend my money on. If they want me to ride, they can pay me."

As amazing as it may sound, the cowboy actually has to pay an entrance fee to participate in a bull-riding event. If the cowboy is good enough to complete the eight-second ride and has high score, he has a chance at winning the prize money. If the cowboy is bucked off before the end of eight-seconds, he leaves the rodeo arena less his entry fee. All he has to show for his troubles are sore muscles, and a mouth full of dirt. Even though I did think it was crazy that the cowboy had to pay to ride, the money was not the real reason I did not want to ride. The truth was I was scared to ride a bull. The thought of straddling across a raging bull's back while holding on by one hand to a thin rope struck real fear in me. While I might not consider myself brave, I could say I was smart.

After several months of my friends ribbing me about not riding a bull, Larry finally challenged me, "If you are too cheap to pay to ride a bull, I will pay your entrance fee for you. If you win, then you split the pot with me. But, I don't think it's about the money. I think you're chicken."

Larry had pushed my back against the wall; I had no choice but to accept his challenge by responding, "Get your money out and pay the entrance fee," I said. "I am ready to ride a bull. It is about time you guys put up and shut up. Give me your money and I'll go sign up for my bull".

As I walked slowly toward the rodeo event office, fear welled inside me. I thought to myself, *What if I draw a bull like Bodacious?* Bodacious was referred to by many people as "The World's Most Dangerous Bull." He was a huge 2000 lb crossbreed that could make moves that no cowboy could anticipate. He was black as a moonless night, and he was mean to the bone. At the big rodeo in Houston, he nearly killed one of the best bull riders in the sport. In Las Vegas he threw his head back and made a mess of the face of a world champion cowboy. Bodacious was retired in his prime because they were afraid he would eventually kill a cowboy; so I did not have to worry about drawing him. *But, I wondered, what if I drew a bull just as mean?*

I wanted to dart and run, the thought of getting on a bull even half as mean as Bodacious scared me. However, I had to act tough and see this through. My honor was at stake, and I was willing to suffer bodily injury to protect it. No matter what bull I drew, this was going to be my Bodacious ride.

The rodeo event office was crowded with cowboys standing near the event table signing release forms and handing over their cash. I never liked taking part in anything that required me to sign a release form, especially one that included the phrase, "In the event of death, Hard Knocks Rodeo Productions is held harmless and without claim." However, it was too late now to back out so I scribbled my signature with a shaky hand across the bottom of the release form and slid my money to an old cowboy nicknamed "Sledge" sitting behind the table. Sledge turned his head and spit snuff juice on the floor. Then he reached into a box and pulled out an 8 x 11 paper sign that had the number 75 in large black numbers on it. "Pin this sign on your back, then hang around and listen for your number. We will draw in about five minutes, and when we call your number along with the bull's name, that will be your bull. Good luck partner, you will need it. There are some bad bulls in the pen tonight." I could have gone all evening without Sledge's words of "encouragement."

Outside the door of the rodeo event office, Sledge climbed into the bed of the pickup truck and hollered out to all the cowboys. "Okay cowboys, listen up. I will call your number and the bull one time. You miss it, and you don't ride tonight. So listen good."

Spitting a big stream of snuff juice from his mouth, Sledge began to call out the bull draws. Sledge shouted at the top of his lungs reading off number by number and bull by bull, I was hoping there was a mix up in the paperwork and they had lost my number. Finally, Sledge shouted, "Number 75 draws Son of Bo."

One of my friends slapped me on the back and said, "Boy, you sure know how to pick em! Son of Bo has mean blood in him, his daddy was Bodacious, and he is an ornery son of a gun." I could not believe what I was hearing; this whole bull-riding thing was turning into my greatest nightmare. *The son of Bodacious "The World's Most Dangerous Bull" is the bull I drew for my first ride?* This had to be some kind of bizarre joke. The way things turned out in reality, meant this was going to be my Bodacious Ride.

After the drawing, an older, rugged looking cowboy approached me and extended his rough right hand to shake mine, "Hello cowboy, my name is T.D. I understand you drew Son of Bo."

Shaking his hand with a firm grip I replied, "Good to meet you T.D. You're right, I did draw Son of Bo. Do you know anything about Son of Bo? This is my first ride, and I would appreciate any tips you could give me about him."

T.D. grinned big and said, "Son of Bo, I know a lot about him. I have drawn that bull six times. Up until a few weeks ago, Son of Bo had never been ridden the full eight seconds. I am not trying to scare you, but that bull has bad blood in him and is mean to the bone. He has hurt many cowboys, and some cowboys even refuse to ride him. I just met you cowboy, but if you want to trade bulls, I will take Son of Bo and give you my draw, Red Pepper. Not to brag, but I am the only cowboy to ride Son of Bo the full eight and I swore I would never get on him again. However, if you want to make a trade, I am willing to take him one last time. Nobody would think any less of you if you made the trade."

26

I stood there for what seemed like a long time, considering T.D.'s offer. Moved by his sincere and concerned offer, I wanted to jump at it. After all, this was my first bull. I appreciated the fact that T.D. would be willing to trade bulls and risk his safety for my benefit; he had to be a caring man with a big heart to make such an offer. With all the courage I could muster I replied, "You don't know how much I appreciate your offer T.D., and I know that I should take you up on it. But I am going to stick with Son of Bo."

T.D. placed his hand on my shoulder and said, "Keep your eye on his head. Whichever way he turns his head is where he will go next. Lean back as far as you can, and stay away from his horns, because he will try to throw his head back and catch you with 'em. Dig your spurs in when you come out of the chute, because he will make a hard left turn on you. Be careful cowboy, that bull is as mean as his daddy and has hurt a lot of cowboys." T.D. shook my hand, then turned and walked away toward the bull riding chutes.

I stood over the bucking chute, stared down at the wide back and long horns of Son of Bo, took a deep breath, and then lowered myself into the chute and onto the huge bull. When my butt made contact with Son of Bo, he lunged forward and attempted to climb out of the chute with me on his back. I almost fell backward under the bull, but I felt a strong hand grab me under my arm, and I was pulled from the bull and over the fence to safety. Looking up, I discovered T.D. was the one who had reached down in the chute and pulled me to safety. T.D. patted me on the back and said, "You will be okay cowboy. Just let him settle down."

As Son of Bo continued to buck and pitch in the chute, another cowboy standing over the chute blurted out, "As soon as he settles down a little, climb back on em' and show him you're in control. Slap him hard between the horns, and show him you'll kick his butt if he doesn't settle down."

T.D. looked at me and said, "Don't listen to him, he has either had too much to drink or has taken a few too many kicks in the head. Just let him settle down, lean back, and dig your spurs in."

Son of Bo settled down, although he continued to snort and paw the ground. When I lowered myself down he again protested being in the chute with me on his back. I grabbed the bull rope in my left hand, slid my right hand in the handhold on the bull rope, and wrapped my hand with the end of the rope. I pushed my hat down on my head, dug my spurs into Son of Bo's side, gave a nod, and said, "Let him go boys."

The gate on the chute burst open and all hell broke loose. Son of Bo twisted to the right, and jumped from the chute with all four feet off the ground. My shoulder was nearly pulled out of socket when the raging bull hit the ground and made a hard twisting cut to the left. The momentum from the twisting turn tossed me off center and to the right side as Son of Bo threw his head and large horns back nearly hitting me in the face. As the killer bull jumped back to the right and kicked his hind legs straight up, I was tossed head-first from his back with my hand still stuck in the bull rope handhold. Hung up in the rigging, Son of Bo continued to buck wildly dragging me in tow. He hooked one of my legs in his horns and tossed me in the air, pulling my hand free from the bull rope handhold. I landed hard with my face in the dirt and the rodeo clowns quickly moved in front of Son of Bo to divert him from me. Dazed from the hard fall, I crawled away, trying to get on my feet. I scrambled toward the arena fence with Son of Bo, his head down, in hard pursuit. Before I could reach the safety of the fence, Son of Bo butted me in the rear and lifted my feet off the ground tossing me hard into the fence. The crushing impact into the fence stunned me momentarily. As I struggled to climb the fence, a strong hand grabbed me by the back of my shirt and pulled me over the top of the fence. As I went over the fence to safety, Son of Bo crashed into the fence in one final effort to get his revenge.

I sat on the ground stunned. As I tried to regain my senses, I heard the announcer over the loud speaker tell the crowd, "Give that cowboy a big hand, because your applause is all he will take home tonight, other than the dirt on his face and sore muscles."

"Cowboy, I think you made Son of Bo mad," said T.D. as he patted me on the back.

"T.D., did you reach down and pull me over the fence?" I ask struggling to get my breath.

"Well you looked like you were in a storm, so I gave you a little help getting over the fence," T.D. replied with a grin.

"Thanks, T.D. I really appreciate your help," I told him as he pulled me to my feet.

My first attempt at riding a bull did not go too well, and I was lucky my pride was all I had injured. Determined to redeem my pride, I got on more bulls over the next few months. Each time I rode, I learned a little more and even made the full eight on a couple of them.

However, I will always remember my last bull ride and the shouts of the crowd when I completed the full eight. Afterwards, I climbed over the arena fence to get away from the raging bull and felt a hand on the back of my shirt pulling me over the top. T.D. the same old cowboy who had helped me on my first ride, once again pulled me to safety. With a big grin on his face and a slap on my back, T.D. said, "Congratulations, you're now the second cowboy to ride Son of Bo the full eight."

Shaking his hand, I replied, "I am proud to be in your company T.D."

To Rodeo, You Have to Pay the Entry Fee

To participate in a rodeo you have to pay the entry fee and the same thing applies in life. To pursue your bodacious opportunities, you must be willing to pay the "entry fee" and accept the bodacious draws, which are opportunities. Bodacious opportunities are those that will scare you, so the entry fee isn't necessarily money, but courage, hard work, and extraordinary commitment. Bodacious opportunities will stretch you beyond your comfort zone and into areas you might normally not venture, if you are willing to pay the fee.

Too often, we fail to realize our dreams because we are not willing to pay the entry fee or tap into our courage. Instead of living extraordinary, unrestrained, and bold lives, we make excuses. We rationalize, instead of having the courage to pursue a bodacious opportunity that has a higher element of risk. Only when we are willing to pay the entry fee of extraordinary commitment, unrestrained action, and bold execution can we begin the path to realizing our dreams.

I failed on my first attempt to ride Son of Bo and experienced several other failures before I finally rode a bull the full eight seconds. Along the way, I bucked off many more bulls than I rode the full eight seconds. You too can expect to "buck off" more times than you succeed along the way to conquering your bodacious opportunities and realizing your big dreams. Do not quit before you conquer your bodacious opportunities. When you buck off, get up off the ground, dust yourself off, and take on the next bodacious opportunity. Bodacious opportunities may only come along once in life, so you may have only one chance to take the ride or opt out. I encourage you to pay the fee and take the bodacious ride.

BODACIOUS RELATIONSHIPS

In bull riding, the fall from the bull is usually painful and uncontrolled. When the bull launches you from his back, where you are going to land and how you will land are out of your control. One thing you do know to do is run, crawl, or scramble the best you can to get out of the way of the bull that is looking for a piece of you.

Relationships with other people, particularly people we care the most about, can be a bodacious ride at times. These bodacious relationships can bring us our most joy and in turn bring us the most pain. Too often with people whom we care the most about, we desire control of the relationship. We become frustrated when the relationships seem out of control, just like a fall off of a bucking bull.

Bodacious relationships require extraordinary commitment, unrestrained action, and bold dedication. Relationships will not always be perfect and those closest to you will fail you at times. However, when you fail or someone close to you fails you, be willing to get up off the ground and scramble to make it right. Shake off the pain of the fall, knock the dirt and dust of disappointment and pride off; have the courage to extend a helping hand and forgiveness to those who fail you. Be bodacious, and build extraordinary, unrestrained, and bold relationships. To realize your most bodacious relationship opportunities you must foster and grow relationships with those close to you.

When a cowboy is bucked off a bull, he is in danger and can be injured seriously if the bull gores him or runs over him. When a cowboy is dazed and confused by the fall he is at high risk of injury from the bull and needs someone to help him. The rodeo clown's job is to distract the bull from the cowboy long enough for the cowboy to get to safety. The clown risks his own safety for the well-being of the cowboy who has fallen to the ground. You too will need a "clown," someone who you can count on to be there when you have been knocked hard to the ground by relationships or circumstances in life. You will need someone who is willing to give you support and is there when you have taken a hard fall.

The first time I rode a bull, T.D. was there to help, coach, encourage, and rescue me. When one of the other cowboys working the chute gave bad advice to hit Son of Bo between the ears, T.D. was quick to correct the advice. After I bucked off, T.D. was there to pull me over the fence to safety and give me an encouraging pat on the back. As you pursue your bodacious opportunities, you will need a clown or a T.D.; someone capable of giving sound advice; an encourager, and a rescuer. Unfortunately, too many people give bad advice or fail to encourage when you make a mistake. A clown is a rare find. Here are the qualities a good clown will possess.

- *Experience:* This is not their first rodeo; they are educated and proven by experience.

- *Wisdom:* They have the wisdom to dispense their knowledge and do so without the expectation of personal gain. Their advice is born out of experience and wisdom rather than out of emotion.

- *Encouragement:* They cheer you on when you are the underdog and fuel your courage to move to the next challenge. They motivate you when you are down and encourage you to be extraordinary, unrestrained, and bold.

- *Loyalty:* They are beside you in your most troubling times; they extend a hand and pull you up.

A good clown is a rare find, and the best way to find a clown is to be a clown yourself. If you go out looking for a clown, you may not find one. If you go out determined to be a clown, you will find many. So, make the deliberate decision to be a clown to someone else and create extraordinary, unrestrained, and bold relationships.

THE EIGHT-SECOND RULE

In rodeo, if a cowboy bucks off his bull in seven seconds he receives no score. The only chance to win is riding the full eight seconds. The shortfall may be only one second, but the cowboy losses his entry fee and any opportunity for the prize money. One second makes a big difference in bull riding, and small things make a difference if you desire to live a bodacious life.

The eight-second rule also applies to life and our pursuit of our dreams. In bull riding, there is no score for the bull you do not ride, or the bull ridden only for seven seconds. It is impossible to achieve a dream or live bodaciously if you never pursue bodacious opportunities or give up too soon. You do not realize profits in business for a sale that was almost made. Life-long goals and lasting relationships are missed by not living courageously. Too often, we quit on our opportunities and relationships with only one second remaining. All too often, just as we are close to going the full eight, we give up. To live bodaciously, you have to go the full eight! To go the full eight you must have extraordinary commitment, unrestrained action, and bold execution.

Once the cowboy bucks off, he does not get a second chance to ride the same bull the same day. However, he does have the option to pay his entry fee at the next rodeo and get on another bull. In pursuit of our dreams, we will come close to succeeding in bodacious opportunities only to "buck-off" with one second to go. We succeed at our dreams not because we are successful in each opportunity, but because we get up off the ground, pay another entry fee, and pursue the next bodacious opportunity.

There will be times you will fail to be the type person you should be. Do not stop trying just because you fail once; or even more than once. Get up and pay the entry fee again. To be a successful bull rider, the cowboy must look at what he did wrong after each ride and then make corrections on the next ride. The same applies to failed relationships and opportunities; look at what you did wrong instead of focusing on what the other person did wrong to you. Pay the entry fee, make corrections, and try again. A cowboy will never ride a bull that he does not get on, and you will never grow a relationship with someone you never spend time being around.

A complete bull ride is a full eight seconds; not seven seconds. If you want to have full "eight-second" bodacious relationships, you must commit time to developing the relationship. To get to know someone and develop a full and meaningful relationship, there is no substitute for time spent with another person. Only when you commit to spend time with someone will you experience a full eight-second bodacious relationship.

Go the full eight seconds in relationships and opportunities; get up off the ground when you fail; pay the entry fee, and try it again.

If I had not got on Son of Bo and gave it my best the first time, I would have never realized the dream of eventually riding him the full eight seconds in the future.

So go ahead and make the bodacious ride! It may be your only opportunity to go the full eight, in a relationship or an opportunity.

BODACIOUS ACTION REQUIRED

- Be willing to pay the entry fee of extraordinary commitment, unrestrained action and, bold execution

- Have the courage to take the bodacious ride

- Pursue bodacious relationships

- You need a clown with Experience, Wisdom, Encouragement, and Loyalty

- Be a clown and you will find a clown

- Apply the Eight Second Rule and make the full ride every time

CHAPTER FOUR

Stop Catching Chickens

STOP CATCHING CHICKENS

 MY FATHER TOLD ME TO "WORK HARD AND BE honest in all your dealings." This was good advice from a hard working and honest man whom I hold in high respect. Honesty and the willingness to work hard are strong foundations for extraordinary commitment, unrestrained action, and bold execution.

My first real job at the age of thirteen was working on a chicken catching crew. This job was an important learning experience for me and helped me to form a question I still ask myself on a regular basis, "Am I catching chickens or eating chicken?"

HOW TO CATCH A CHICKEN

I love to eat fried chicken, good crispy fried chicken. Restaurant style chicken and fast food takeout are good, but my favorite is chicken fried at home in a skillet, just like mom cooked most every week when I was growing up. Fried chicken is great, but have you ever given thought to how chickens get from the chicken farm to the grocery store or restaurant? Think about it, the chickens surely do not volunteer to be deep-fried! Someone has to transport the chickens from the farm to the processing plant and then on to the store or restaurant. Most of us have never given thought to these behind the scenes details. We prefer to see chicken as a product packaged and wrapped or prepared for us on our plate. In reality, it requires a lot of work to get the chicken from the chicken farm to the processing plant.

As any thirteen-year-old boy, I was not very smart about realities of the world. I based my decisions not on facts but whims. When I first heard about the job of catching chickens, my vision was that of something grand, something fun, something you could be proud of doing. I was excited to think that you could do something like chicken catching and get paid for it as well. Although the pay of $4.00 a day for chicken catching did seem a little low to me, I thought, "What the heck? It's not every day you get an opportunity to do something as exciting as catching chickens."

A couple of friends told me about the great opportunity to catch chickens and assured me they would talk to the boss and get me on the chicken catching crew. Sure enough, the important connections worked out and I had the job. I was instructed to meet my crew at the feed mill at 5:00 p.m. sharp. Now, I admit to being a little confused as to why we were getting such a late start; I figured we only had two or three hours of daylight remaining and that it would be difficult catching chickens in the dark.

It was my first day on the job, and I wanted to look my best. So I got out my work hat, which was a beat up Stetson with a shortened brim. That old hat looked the part, with a thick layer of ground in dirt and a burnt hole in the top caused by a dropped King Edward Cigar.

This was a real cowboy hat, not a go on a date hat, but a working man's hat and one that I thought looked good. I put on my best pair of worn out work boots. It was important to have a pair of boots that looked the part. I did not want a clean, shiny, polished pair of boots. I wanted boots that looked experienced, and my boots certainly looked the part. They were a well-worn pair of Justin, pointed toe, slant heeled boots; not the best walking or work boots, but they looked good or at least I thought they did.

I arrived early at the designated meeting point, the town feed mill, which provided me with the opportunity to watch the rest of the crew arrive. The Haggert brothers, who had let me in on this great job opportunity, were the type of guys that usually arrived last minute at everything. The seasoned chicken crew arrived shortly after I did, and they were a rough looking group of guys. Of course, they arrived in a large group and besides being big and scary looking; they were loud and rowdy.

Panic started setting in as the group started my way because something deep down was telling me this is not the friendly welcoming committee. As they came closer, I started looking for my escape routes, and planning which way I would run. I could feel the adrenalin, and like an old farm dog could feel the hair standing up on the back of my neck. To my relief, Big Jake and Dub Haggert arrived just in time. Both Big Jake and Dub were intimidating looking fellows. Dub had long hair and a pretty good beard for a fourteen-year-old, and Big Jake was just as his nickname implied, really big and hairy for his age. Even though the Haggert boys were rough looking guys, they had been my friends since we were small kids. It felt so good to have my "protectors" arrive and stand by me. The menacing group of chicken catchers did not appear so threatening to me now. I could tell that my association with the Haggert brothers was going to prove valuable as I watched the group of chicken catchers move on to harass another rookie.

As I looked around at my work associates, I have to admit they were not what I expected. Instead of the hard working cowboy types I had envisioned, these fellows looked like a work group from the county prison. However, I reckoned that the supervisors would be the type that could keep a group like this under control.

Dust boiled up behind a tractor-trailer rig that was heading down the dirt road that lead to the feed mill. I was excited about riding in a big rig truck, I could just imagine myself riding in the customized cab, shifting through all ten gears and blowing the truck horn. When the rig pulled up, to my dismay it was an old, beat-up looking truck, loaded high with chicken coops. It was not the "big rig truck" with the customized cab I had envisioned; instead, it looked more like something reclaimed from the junkyard.

The door of the truck swung open and the driver climbed down the steps to the ground. The driver, J.O. was a rough looking man, with a scared face, dirty cap, and filthy clothes. In a slurred voice, he started calling names of those that would be on his truck. It was hard to understand him because he slurred every word. I could not tell if he was drunk or had some type of speech problem, but I was hoping for the speech problem. Along with the Haggert boys, I got the call to be on J.O.'s chicken truck. We climbed into the cluttered and filthy cab for the ride to the chicken farm. It was cramped seating with J.O. and three boys in the front seat of the truck. To top it off, I had the gearshift between my legs and it got really uncomfortable when J.O. shifted to 5th gear.

After a long hot ride in the cramped cab, the truck came to a stop in front of a long metal barn at the chicken farm. I was ready to get out of the truck cab, since J.O. and the Haggert boys did not place high priority on taking regular bathes or using deodorant. So, after the ride in a hot smelly cab with a gearshift between my legs I was ready to get some fresh air.

When I walked into the large chicken house for the first time, the thousands of white chickens crammed together in one place awed me. It was a sea of chickens, and the smell was overwhelming. It was at this point I realized this job was going to be hot, smelly, hard work. During my brief job orientation session from Big Jake, I learned that our job was to reach under the chickens, and capture them by their legs. Catch four chickens in your right hand and four chickens in your left hand, for a total of eight chickens, not six and not nine, exactly eight. Big Jake continued to explain that after catching eight chickens, we were to take them to the truck and hand them up for loading into the coops. It sounded simple enough, but the chickens really did not want to cooperate. Catching four chickens in each hand proved to be a tough assignment. Catching one chicken was not too hard, but when you opened your hand to catch the second chicken, the first one would wiggle free and warn the others with loud screams. I soon found out that catching the chickens was the nice part of the job; handing them up to the person on the truck was the really nasty part. In order to hand the chickens to the person on the truck you had to lift the clucking, wing flapping chickens high over your head. With the chickens lifted over your head, poop and feathers would rain down on you; it was as if chickens knew this was their last chance to get revenge.

YOUR CHOICE:
CATCH CHICKENS OR EAT CHICKEN

Chicken catching was hard dirty work. Even though I was young and not all that smart, I knew right away that I did not want to make a career of chicken catching. After only a couple of nights working on the chicken catching crew, I made a decision to stop catching chickens. Since my last night on the chicken catching crew, the closest I have come to catching a chicken is carrying my order out of KFC, Popeye's, or Churches.

There are professional chicken catchers; people whom have made a profession out of chicken catching. During my brief stint as a chicken catcher, I asked J.O., the head chicken catcher, how long he had been doing this job. To my disbelief, he told me he had been catching chickens for 33 years. When I asked why he had been a chicken catcher for 33 years, J.O. replied, "It's all I ever knew I could do. The money is okay, so I just kept on doing it." For 33 years, J.O. had assumed this was all he could do; that there was nothing more for him; that he was simply destined to be a chicken catcher.

You have to be on guard not to let "chicken catching" syndrome creep into your life. This syndrome keeps you doing what is "dirty," unsatisfying, and exhausts you. Chicken catching syndrome is what you do, because you "have to" and not in response to what you are passionate about or inspires you. The first step in moving from being a chicken catcher and becoming a chicken eater is to recognize the chicken catching aspects in your life. These may be hard to identify, because you might be like J.O. the professional chicken catcher who kept on catching chickens because, he accepted it as the best he could do.

Maybe, you have a "chicken catching" job that you have stuck with far too long. The job that you dread going to every day, where at the end of the day you feel like a chicken catcher lifting your catch over your head for the poop to rain down on you. Your day ends leaving you feeling underpaid, underappreciated, and covered with the poop of frustration.

Maybe you are stuck in a chicken catching routine of getting up, fighting traffic, going to work, leaving work, fighting traffic, coming home, eating dinner, turning on the television, and falling asleep on the couch. Your chicken catching routine plays out day after day as the poop of sameness and boredom rains down on you.

Possibly, you continue with chicken catching habits that you have failed to break. Maybe you continue to make unwise decisions in your personal life, or you continue to make poor decisions with your diet and health. You may struggle with maintaining relationships that you failed to develop and nurture, or you remain steadfast in stubbornness refusing to offer forgiveness. Regardless of what your chicken catching syndrome may be, at the end of the day, week, month, year, or lifetime the poop of regret rains down on you for your failure to break the chicken catching syndrome.

THE DIFFERENCE

If you think like a chicken catcher, you will act like a chicken catcher and you will accept ordinary, restrained, and cautious as the path you take. It is quite simple; you will act as you think. A chicken catching mentality will cause you to act in a negative non-productive manner. On the other hand, a chicken eating mentality will cause you to act in an extraordinary, unrestrained, and bold way. Your way of thinking and your viewpoint of the world will determine your actions and the opportunities you will pursue. To help you out, I have listed the key attributes that are essential to live an extraordinary, unrestrained, and bold life. It is your choice to act on these attributes; how you think will determine how you act, and that determines the opportunities you pursue.

HOW TO TELL IF YOU ARE A CHICKEN CATCHER OR CHICKEN EATER

HOW DO YOU LOOK AT...	THE CHICKEN CATCHER VIEWPOINT	THE CHICKEN EATER VIEWPOINT
Commitment	Ordinary	Extraordinary
Action	Restrained	Unrestrained
Execution	Cautious	Bold
Opportunities	Limited, fearful of new opportunities	Abundant, pursues new opportunities
Change	Avoids and fears change, enjoys sameness	Creates and embraces change
Direction	Complains about current situation	Charts their own course
Decisions	Delays making decisions	Makes intentional decisions
Work	Content with doing dirty work	Willing to work hard but desires to work smart
Value	Expects others to bring value to them	Brings value to others
Self Awareness	They are what they are and not much can be done to change it	Realize they have room for personal improvement
Personal Growth	Does not engage in learning	Never stops learning

How Do You Look At...	The Chicken Catcher Viewpoint	The Chicken Eater Viewpoint
Responsibility	Avoids taking responsibility	Takes personal responsibility
Initiative	Low	High
Productivity	Low	High

OPPORTUNITY VIEWPOINT

People with chicken catching syndrome have a limited opportunity viewpoint of their world. They tend to see the world as a place where there is not enough for everyone. A world where opportunities are limited and available only to a few lucky people, gifted people, rich people, smart people, tall people, pretty people, thin people, or any other type of person that meets their self-described exclusivity list. By accepting these self-imposed limitations and exclusions, they take their place at a life table where there is not enough for everyone. You might hear them say things like, "The rich get richer and the poor get poorer" or "I hate this job, but it's the best I can do."

Chicken catchers view the world as a place where only a select group of people can succeed, and they choose to exclude themselves from seeking more opportunity. At the root of this thinking is laziness and fear. Chicken catchers are too lazy and fearful to explore and dream about greater opportunities or pursue opportunities placed before them.

Years ago, I made my decision to stop catching chickens and become extraordinary, unrestrained, and bold. However, people with chicken catching syndrome continue to do the dirty work and

ᴜt the poop raining down on them. They have bought
that there is nothing more in life for them, and they are
ᴛo pursue other opportunities. Chicken catchers believe the
ᴀt there are no more opportunities available to people like them
ᴅ accept their miserable lot in life. When I catch myself thinking
that I have reached my pinnacle of achievement, I recall the time
when I walked away from catching chickens and discovered larger
opportunities. It starts with your decision to stop catching chickens
and your decision to be extraordinary, unrestrained, and bold.

CHICKEN EATERS ARE EXTRAORDINARY, UNRESTRAINED, AND BOLD

After making my decision to stop catching chickens, I worked as a
farm hand, hauled hay, milked cows and worked as a ranch hand.
From the time, I was thirteen years old I have had a job of some type.
When I was a young man, my goal was to become a top cowboy.
However, I can recall the hot long days working on the ranch and
daydreaming about going to college and having a professional job.
Because I had no idea about how to get into a college or what type
of professional job to pursue, I never spoke about my dream. I feared
that my friends might have laughed at me if I told them my big secret
dream. After all, we did not know anyone who had left our small
town, attended college, or pursued a professional career. People in
this small town were blue-collar working, big-hearted folks whom
were some of the best people you would ever meet. However, I had
a deep desire to pursue a vastly different path for my life; I wanted
to do something different. At times, I would try to convince myself I
liked working on a ranch and that I really wanted to make it my life.
While I knew other people who did live their dream by working on
a ranch, deep down inside me I knew that I wanted something different, even though I did not know exactly what it was.

It is strange how we want to convince ourselves we are happy with being ordinary, restrained, and cautious in our life. If you remain complacent and deny your dreams or yourself, after a while the fire of your big dream will dim and will eventually be extinguished. Keep your dream alive by believing you can do more. Believe you can live your dream by being extraordinary, unrestrained, and bold. Do not settle for chicken catching, be a chicken eater.

A GOOD OPPORTUNITY IS NOT ALWAYS THE BEST OPPORTUNITY

A few months after Mattie and I were married, I was offered a job working on a large ranch that raised registered cattle. The job included a rent-free house. It sat on a hill overlooking a large lake that stretched for several miles and a new pickup truck to drive. To top it all off, there was a beautiful ski boat that was ours to use when the owner was not at the ranch. The job responsibilities included caring for the expensive show cattle and overseeing the ranch property. In addition to these duties, during the stock show season, Mattie and I would travel all expenses paid, to take the best cattle to the various stock shows and fairs around the country. For a newly married young couple this was an exciting opportunity to travel, and have our housing, recreation, and transportation needs provided for in one package.

At the end of my interview, the ranch owner indicated the job was mine if I wanted it. He told me to talk it over with Mattie and call him the next day to let him know if I wanted the job. As we drove out of the gate of the ranch to head back home, both of us were excited about the new opportunity. The ranch was beautiful; the house was perfect, and the job was the pinnacle of what I wanted to achieve as a cowboy. That night I was so excited about the new job that I had trouble sleeping. Knowing a full day of work lie ahead of me on the ranch where I was currently working, I did my best to get some sleep. That morning during breakfast, Mattie and I talked about the new job with excitement. Mattie liked the house and was already talking about ways she could put her touches on it. The new truck and traveling to the fair and stock shows really got me excited.

I finished breakfast and kissed Mattie, then I headed out the door for work. During the drive that morning, I rehearsed what I would say when I called my prospective new boss to accept the job. At the same time, I was concerned how I would tell the ranch foreman where I currently worked that I would be leaving.

TAKE THIS JOB AND SHOVEL IT

I drove through the ranch's main gate and it immediately became evident that I had a tough day ahead of me as soon as I saw a trac-tor-trailer loaded with cotton hulls that sat outside the barn. Cotton hulls are used as filler in the cattle feed and need to be stored inside a barn and protected from the rain. Cotton hulls are difficult to handle because of the way they stick together; auger systems simply dig a tunnel in the hulls instead of moving them. The only way to get cotton hulls unloaded from the truck to the barn would be to shovel them, one shovel load at a time. Climbing from the pick-up truck, I asked the truck driver to back the trailer into the barn, drop the trailer and I would call when it was unloaded.

It was early morning, but the Texas sun was already beating down and it was stifling hot. Inside the barn where the trailer was dropped, there was little air movement and it was like an oven with the hot sun beating down on the tin roof. Cotton hulls are not heavy to shovel, but they are extremely dirty and dusty. As I shoveled the cotton hulls, thick dust mixed with my sweat and covered my entire body and clothes with a layer of filth. All day I shoveled hulls from the back of the trailer. I only took a few breaks, and by the end of the day; I was drained from the heat, covered in dust, and exhausted.

I sat down to evaluate my work. I was proud that less than half the trailer load remained in the front of the trailer. Exhausted and drained from the heat, I decided to stop for the day and finish first thing in the morning. Climbing from the trailer, I remembered I had not told my boss that I would be leaving to take another job. I wanted to make sure I told him before leaving for the day and assure him I would be back to finish shoveling the remaining hulls before I moved on. Walking from the barn into the cool breeze, I was met by the ranch foreman, who was a rugged, grouchy individual who could be very difficult to get along with at times. Even though he was a difficult person, I liked the old fellow and most of the time we got along well.

The foreman took one look inside the truck and snapped back, "You been playing around all day? Anyone worth their pay could have shoveled the entire truck in a day and still have time left over."

His comments caught me by surprise and really struck a nerve. Before thinking, I tossed the shovel to the foreman and replied, "Being you're so good, you can shovel the rest of them. I think you would be happier with someone else, so I will not be back in the morning."

As I walked from the barn to my truck, the foreman gave me a good cussing and "accepted my resignation."

On the drive home, I began to worry that I had just quit my job and did not officially have the new job. Mattie and I lived on a very tight budget and missing even one of day work would be devastating. What if I called the ranch owner and discovered he had changed his mind? I regretted my abrupt reaction to the ranch foreman *What if I had to go back and ask for him a job? Would he let me have my old job back?* Even if he did give the job back, I knew there would be hell to pay.

Choose the Extraordinary, Unrestrained and Bold Route

As I drove along the country road that led from the ranch to the main highway, I continued to think about the job I had just quit. There were many things I liked about the cowboy life and working on ranches. The people were genuine and down to earth, and I enjoyed the wide-open spaces and slower pace. On the other hand, it was hard, dirty work and held little opportunities for career growth. The real question that I had to answer was, "When would I come clean with myself and follow my big dream of attending college, and pursuing a professional career? When would I trade my cowboy boots and jeans for dress shoes and slacks? When would I trade the wide-open spaces and pursue my dream of a corner office? Did accepting the next ranch job move me closer to realizing my big dream?"

I pressed on the brake firmly and my pickup came to a stop at the crossroad of the main highway. I sat at the crossroad and faced a decision, should I take the usual route along the same highway I traveled everyday or should I take the less familiar scenic route? In a similar way, I was at a crossroad in life with my career decision. Should I turn left onto the familiar road of another ranch job, or would I have the courage to take the extraordinary, unrestrained, and bold route?

I usually turned left to take the shortest way home; however, that day I decided to turn right and take the longer more scenic road home. Cool wind blew through the open window of the truck as I drove along the winding river road through the rugged Texas hills.

Dust boiled from beneath the truck as I pulled off to the side of the road at a scenic overlook point. I walked to the edge of the overlook then sat down on a large rock. Positioned at this high point of the overlook, I could see the countryside stretching to the far away horizon. Beyond the horizon was my big dream. I realized that if I wanted to clearly see that dream as more than a hazy far off image, I would have to venture out to the horizon to see what lay beyond it. I decided to be extraordinary, unrestrained, and bold. I stood up ready to take the first step toward my personal horizon, steps that would lead me to discover new paths that would lead to my big dream.

The first step is always the biggest and most difficult. For the first time I realized that if I wanted to pursue my big dream, I must turn down the new ranch job and find another job that did not involve cattle ranching or farming. Working on farms or ranches was all I had ever done, so that was as far as I could see on the horizon. I had no idea what was beyond the horizon of farming and ranching, but I knew I needed to go beyond the horizon so I could see more.

I climbed back into the pick-up truck and continued my drive home, all the while wondering what I could do if it was not ranching or farming. Maybe I could work in a store, factory, or maybe learn a trade? The winding country road ended at the main highway and I turned left and headed home along the busy highway. I made this familiar drive everyday; however, today a large factory building that I had passed many times caught my attention. A large sign in front of the building advertised "Hiring Loading Dock Workers." Without pause, I turned my truck into the parking lot of the factory. As I drove slowly through the parking lot, I spotted a man who was wearing a white dress shirt and tie walking to his car. I rolled down the truck's window and asked him, "Excuse me sir, do you know who I need to see to apply for the loading dock job?"

"Sure do cowboy, you're looking at him. Are you interested in working on a loading dock?" Without a second thought I answered, "Yes, sir, I am. I don't know anything about working on a loading dock, but I am willing to work hard and learn." All he had to do was look in the window of my truck to see I was covered with dirt from a hard day of work.

"Good, you may be just the man we are looking for. Come see me at 8:00 a.m. tomorrow morning, and we can talk about it. My name is Richard Crowley but just ask for Rich when you come in tomorrow."

WHEN YOU COME TO THE CROSSROADS IN YOUR LIFE

At the crossroads of life, take the extraordinary, unrestrained and bold route. It may be longer and not as straight, but it will lead to your horizon.

- Resist the temptation to be ordinary, restrained, and to play it safe.
- Your big dream lies beyond the horizon of what you can see today.
- Take the first step, go to your horizon, and then you will be able to see more.
- Explore new routes that may lead to your dream.
- Write down your big dream.
- Walk away from your "chicken catching" activity.
- Be extraordinary, unrestrained, and bold; go to the horizon of what you can see today and you will see more.

COURAGE TO PURSUE THE BIG DREAM

The next morning at breakfast, I told Mattie that I was going to apply for a job on a loading dock, and if I got it I would not take the ranch job. It was difficult to tell her because I knew she wanted the little ranch house on the hill overlooking the lake. In her supportive way, Mattie took my hand and told me that she hoped I got the job I wanted. Knowing Mattie was willing to give up what she wanted made me realize how blessed I was to have a loving and supportive wife. Without her support and encouragement along the way, I might not have pursued my dream. It is important that the people closest to you are willing to make the journey with you toward your big dream.

That morning after a short interview with Rich he said, "The job on the loading dock is yours. When can you start?"

"I can start this morning, if you can put me to work," I replied without hesitation.

Surprised at my response, Rich replied, "This morning? I have never had anyone want to start work the same day they got the job. However, I think we can work that out. Let me take you to the dock and introduce you to your new boss."

Turning down the ranch job was a hard thing to do. Everything about the job seemed so good, with one exception. It would not put me on the path to my big dream. Reflecting back, turning down the ranch job was the best decision, I ever made. It was a difficult decision to turn down a good opportunity in order to pursue my best opportunity and my big dream.

Shortly after getting the loading dock job, I learned the company benefits program would pay tuition and books for me to attend college. When I worked as a cowboy, I wondered how I would be able to afford the cost of attending college, and now, to my amazement, the problem was solved, and in a way I could not see until I went beyond my horizon. The next three years, I worked all day and attended college at night. It made for long days for me, but even longer days for Mattie who cared for our new baby girl.

One day while driving my forklift, Rich stepped out in the aisle, waving his arms to flag me down. It had been a while since I had visited with Rich, but we seemed to make a connection the day he hired me. I stopped my forklift beside Rich and turned the noisy engine off so we would not have to scream over the noise.

He extended his hand as I stepped from the forklift. Rich said, "I've noticed you've been going to night school for some time now. Have you learned anything?"

I was puzzled by the abrupt question but replied, "Sure have, I am working on my engineering degree. Someday I will design the equipment I load here every day."

Rich continued, "I am sure you noticed the new units we've been loading onto flatbed trucks lately. These are the largest most complex units we have ever made; and we need someone to travel to the job sites to startup and commission these large units. We have watched how you have progressed since you have been with the company, and we believe you would be the right man for the job. What do you think?"

Dumbfounded, I replied, "I must be dreaming, Rich. Are you sure that I am the man for the job?"

Again he extended his right hand for a handshake of agreement. "I've never been so sure about anything. If you are interested, you start factory consultant training next week."

I thrust my hand into his and almost pulled his arm out of the socket as I shook it like a wild man. "Rich, I can't tell you how much I thank you for this opportunity. I will not let you down."

As Rich walked away toward the front office, I stood beside my forklift shocked and excited. I could not wait to get home and tell Mattie about the new job.

The factory consultant job required traveling around the country to oversee final commissioning of the largest and most complex products manufactured by the company. While I really enjoyed the new job, and the pay increase was a big boost, I spent a lot of time on the road and many nights out. I missed being at home with Mattie and our daughter. Mattie was pregnant with our second child and it was hard on her when I was not home all week. The travel complicated my home life and was a big obstacle to my college work. Because of the extensive travel, I was unable to continue my college coursework and earn an engineering degree. However, I was learning a lot in my new job and I was willing to put my college on temporary hold. The factory consultant job was the launching pad for my career, because it could lead to jobs as a sales representative, in sales management, and eventually into senior management levels.

All this opportunity started at the crossroad at the moment I chose the extraordinary, unrestrained, and bold route instead of the familiar route. I went to my personal horizon and when I got there, I could see a little further. The day I sat on the rock at the overlook and looked over the horizon I never imagined all this opportunity was just beyond what I could see.

Years ago when I ask Rich for a job on the loading dock, I just wanted to pursue my big dream. I never considered I might be sitting in a corner office someday, and never dreamed that I would own a business of this size. It is a long way from working as a cowboy to working as a senior executive and finally owning the company I worked in for many years.

When the founding owner of the company died suddenly, I was appointed by the family to run the business. After a few years of running the company, the opportunity to own the company was presented to me. This big bodacious opportunity scared me just as much as my first ride on Son of Bo. To acquire the company required that I put everything I owned on the line. It was a tough ride at first, during the first year of ownership I made some big mistakes and almost went broke.

As you can see, the company survived and it just goes to show, that what lies beyond the horizon of what you can see today can be much greater than you ever dreamed. To see what is beyond your horizon you must choose the extraordinary, unrestrained, and bold route. If you take the journey and stay the course, you'll be on your way to realizing your big dream.

Unrestrained Action Required

- Choose the extraordinary, unrestrained, and bold route

- Know when you are catching chickens and take the first step to stop

- Do not leave one chicken catching activity and exchange it for another

- Have the courage to turn down good opportunities and pursue your best opportunities

- Go to your horizon where you will be able to see beyond the now

- Make the decision, stay on course, and pursue your big dream

CHAPTER FIVE

Extraordinary, Unrestrained and Bold Leadership

MOVE YOUR HERD GENTLY

WHEN I WORKED ON THE RANCH, I WOULD GET out of bed an hour or more before everyone else so I could just spend time alone in the quiet stillness of the morning. Early morning was my favorite time on the ranch; the cool morning air and the quietness provided a good setting for personal reflection. This was the time when no one else was awake; it was just the quiet stillness and me; and I could spend my time in prayer. Setting aside the first part of each day to reflect and pray is important to me and starts my day in the right way.

I recall one morning when my quiet time was cut short by the need to start work earlier than normal. We needed to get ready for a long horseback ride to the back pastures in the canyon lands of the ranch. The cows and calves ranged in the open pastures and needed to be brought in so each cow and calf could be checked and doctored. Moving cattle long distances during the heat of the day was hard on the cattle and the horses, so it was important for us to get an early start.

After riding a couple of hours in the pre-dawn darkness, we found the herd bedded down in a grove of trees near a small creek. Arnold, the ranch owner, dismounted his horse and said to the group of four cowboys, "Boys, get off your horses, and let's talk just a minute." The four of us were a little surprised that he wanted to talk. It was out of character for Arnold to spend time talking instead of working. Regardless, he was the boss, so we dismounted our horses and moved close to Arnold. "Boys, a couple of you have ridden with me before and a couple of you haven't," he said. For those of you who have not ridden with me before, I want to make sure you know how to move the herd. For you two boys who have ridden with me, I want to remind you."

Being a young cocky cowboy, I thought to myself, *What can this old man tell me about moving a herd that I don't already know; this isn't the first time I've done this.*

Arnold spit a stream of tobacco juice and continued, "You may think you know everything about moving a herd, and that's fine. You may think I am in the cattle business; well I ain't, I am in the steak business. My business is to provide my customers with the best tasting and most tender steaks possible. That is why we feed corn to our beef cattle and carefully mix the feed. For the same reason, that is why we pasture our cows and calves on the greenest pastures and feed them the best hay. If you want tasty and tender steaks, you have to feed cattle the right food, and move the herd gently. Moving them gently is what I want to make sure you understand before we get started. When moving the herd, if you holler, make them run, scare them, or push them too hard, our customer will not get tender steaks; they will get tough steaks. To produce tender steaks, we must move the herd persistently and gently. Today, there will be no hollering, no running the cattle, and no cracking of the whip. We will get to where we need to go with the herd in the same amount time, if not sooner, by doing it the right way.

The four of you will move the herd, with one man riding point, one driving the rear and the other two on each side. For the point man, you don't have to worry about moving the entire herd where you want them to go; you need to move only the bull and the lead cows in the right direction and the rest of the herd will follow. For you boys on the sides, your job is to keep the herd from spreading out, or they will go off in the wrong direction instead of following the herd. Keep the herd tight and moving as one, but do not push them too hard. For the cowboy bringing up the rear, I have bad news for you. You are going to eat a lot of dust today, because as the herd moves they are going to kick up a lot of dust. Nonetheless, your job is very important because you have to keep the cows in the rear moving forward. As the herd moves forward, the cows in the rear will be tempted to turn back and head to the pasture they just left. I will go after the stray calves that wander from the herd so that we don't have to hold up the entire herd to retrieve one wandering calf."

That day, we moved a large herd of over one hundred cows and calves several miles from the pasture to the main corral. Just as Arnold instructed us, there was no hollering, running the herd, or cracking our whips and the herd moved gently and persistently toward the corral. Arnold was quick to lasso the strays and bring them back into the herd. As for me, I was the unfortunate cowboy bringing up the rear, and it was just as Arnold promised; dirty and dusty. When a cow stopped along the way, she would look back at the pasture we left and attempt to turn back. When we first started on the drive, it was difficult bringing up the rear, because many cows wanted to turn back. However, it got easier the further we went, and when the pasture was no longer in sight, fewer cows attempted to turn back.

LESSONS FROM MOVING THE HERD

The lessons and techniques I learned as a cowboy moving herds of cattle are the same secrets you can apply when leading a team of people. Effective leaders know how to move a team in the right direction and get consistent results. In contrast, ineffective leaders cannot lead a team and only get short-term results. The difference between an effective and ineffective leader is not intelligence, education, pedigree, or resume. The difference lies in their ability to move their herd to the desired destination.

Moving people is much like moving cattle, you must move them gently and the best way to move the herd is to move their leaders. If you move the leaders who are closest to the team, then it is much easier to move the entire herd gently. Attempting to move a team by mandate will only work short term and used long term, will result in a stampede. Be aware there will always be stragglers, the team members who are resistant to change. This group is similar to the cattle in the rear of the herd that want to return to their old pasture. The stragglers want to turn back to their old ways; they are comfortable doing what they are doing and see no reason to change. Be careful not to let the stragglers slow down the herd's momentum. Have someone else round them up and keep them moving, but don't stop the herd to wait on them. People get comfortable with what they are doing and how they do it.

Initiating change in an organization requires that the leader has a clear understanding of what business they are in and a passion for getting to the desired destination. Arnold was in the steak business instead of the cattle business, he was passionate about his business, had clarity in what he wanted to accomplish and how it he would accomplish it.

To lead a team from where they are to where you want them to be, you must:

- Understand what business you are in
- Know where you want to take them
- Be passionate about getting them to the destination
- Communicate with passion the destination, the objectives, and the path. Tell the team where they are going, how they will get there, and the benefits of getting to the destination. It is a common mistake for leaders to call a meeting to communicate their vision and goals, assuming that everyone understands and has bought into the destination and making the trip. Even though everyone may nod their head in agreement, do not believe that they have bought into the destination or making the trip with you. The bigger the change, the bigger the goal, the more you have to communicate. To get everyone on the right path and heading the right direction requires that you over communicate the destination and the path. If you err, err on the side of over communicating; do not assume that everyone is bought in until you see willing action. You will know you are getting through when people stop nodding and start moving. When you move the leaders, you will move the herd. If your leaders have not bought into the destination and the path, they will allow the team to turn back at the first sign of resistance. Realize that part of moving your team forward will require discomfort. People tend to be uncomfortable with change so you should not be surprised when they want to quit and turn back at the first experience of discomfort.

- Your job as a leader is to keep the herd moving forward. The further you move them along the path toward the destination, the less the temptation to turn back persists. By applying the secrets of moving the herd, you can move your team forward in an extraordinary, unrestrained and bold way.

- Be a Bodacious leader and bring value by leading your team to new destinations. Move them gently, but move them forward. Keep them moving forward by moving the leaders and do not be surprised when people complain about being uncomfortable.

- Be an Extraordinary, Unrestrained, and Bold leader by:

- Communicating the destination and the path

- Moving the team by moving the leaders

- Moving the team from comfort to discomfort and toward the destination

- Keep the team moving forward when they are tempted to turn back

Unfortunately, not everyone who is placed in a position of leadership is a Bodacious leader, so let me tell you about another type of leader.

THE PIRATE CODE

Hard work filled our days on the ranch and by evening, the cowboys were ready to relax. Some of the cowboys enjoyed having a few drinks (or a few too many), playing cards, or sitting around telling the same stories over and over. They must have believed that if they told the same lie enough times, then the lie would magically become true. While I was not antisocial with the other cowboys, I did enjoy finding a nice quiet spot where I could enjoy reading a good book. One evening while in the main house, I noticed that Arnold had a small collection of well-worn books tucked away in one corner of his den. One book entitled *Pirate Legends and Stories* caught my eye, so I stood by the bookcase and casually thumbed through the pages.

From across the room Arnold said to me, "If you want to read that old book, it's yours to read. Just bring it back when you are finished." I accepted Arnold's offer and made my way to bunkhouse where I found a quiet corner to read the book. I found the book interesting and full of adventure; I finished it in a couple of days. This was the first book I had read about the Pirates that roamed the Caribbean and up to that point knew little about them. I found it interesting that the Pirates had their own set of codes that governed the ship and its crew. New crewmembers pledged their allegiance to honor the code. A common way to pledge was for the crewmember to place their hand on a human skull and vow their allegiance.

Article I of the Pirates code detailed how the prize, or booty, would be distributed among the officers and the crew.

> **Article I.** *Every Man shall obey civil Command; the Captain shall have one full share and a half of all prizes; the Master, Carpenter, Boatswain and Gunner shall have one share and quarter.*
>
> CAPTAIN JOHN PHILLIPS, Captain of the ship Revenge 1724

While the pirates pledged to a code of how the wealth would be distributed, you must remember that they were pirates and were not too good at following rules. Therefore, it was common practice for the captain and his officers to cheat the crew out of their due share.

The movies and stories tend to romanticize pirates as being a fun-loving group who at times broke a few rules and plundered a few ships. In reality, pirates were takers who made a life of taking from others for their own benefit. They would take from the passing ships, and they would take from one another. The captain's pledge to the crew and the ship was all too often a convenience and often viewed as more of a guideline as opposed to a governing code.

PIRATE LEADERS

There are pirates today, and you may encounter one of them, because all too often they are in positions of leadership. Pirate leaders, like their seagoing cousins, are takers. Pirate leaders choose not to communicate a vision, or plan, because they do not have an ultimate destination that includes the team. The ultimate destination that a pirate leader has is intended to benefit him or her personally.

You regularly hear the words I, me, and mine come from a pirate leader's mouth, because it really is all about them. Driven by personal recognition and compensation, pirate leaders are quick to sacrifice long-term vision for short-term performance that enhances their own recognition and compensation. They lead a team like a pirate captain in possession of a treasure map, and the crew is just along to facilitate finding the treasure that the captain has no intention of sharing. Pirate leaders pillage a team for their selfish benefit and move from organization to organization in search of the next treasure.

Pirate leaders stampede their herd with threats and intimidation. In a pirate led organization, team members are singled out, belittled and made public examples. Threats, humiliation and intimidation are the tools of the pirate leader. They stampede their team by using fear to motivate, which causes people to panic and make poor decisions. As a result, the panicked team makes decisions based on short-term results. Frustration and panic is allowed to rule the stampeding, out of control team, which wants only one thing: to get the pirate leader off their back.

Teamwork dissolves into self-preservation as the pirate leader pushes the team harder toward achievement of his personal goals.

There are many good and bad lists in a pirate lead organization. Those at the top of the good list are safe, but for the poor souls at the bottom of one of the many lists, only public beating and humiliation are guaranteed. A pirate leader has so many lists, that it is common to be on the good list one day and on the bad list the next, or even on both within the same day.

Quality people do not rally behind a pirate leader; they may tolerate them for a little while, but eventually quality people sign on with another crew. The only people who follow pirate leaders are fellow pirates. Organizations lead by pirate leaders operate on the edge of mutiny. Quality people become frustrated and leave while the pirates take over to pillage and plunder the organization. Quality people will not work in an organization led by a pirate leader, and quality organizations do not exist under pirate leadership.

BODACIOUS LEADERS

There is a better way to lead and that is to be a bodacious leader. A bodacious leader is dedicated to creating an extraordinary, unrestrained, and bold team. Bodacious leaders are great communicators; they instill confidence by being genuine and speaking in an honest, open manner and by never using political talk to side step the issues. They are passionate about their vision and understand the importance of transferring their passion for the vision to the team. When people hear them talk about their vision, it is clear they are excited about what they want to achieve and have a plan of action. They carefully communicate the details of their plan and the benefits of achieving the goal.

Bodacious leaders understand that a team is motivated by making the entire team successful, instead of an individual team member or the leader. People follow bodacious leaders because they have a vision, and communicate their vision. Bodacious leaders demonstrate integrity and build trust by acting in alignment with what they say. Good people will follow a person of integrity and character who they can trust. Bodacious leaders build strong teams by surrounding themselves with other bodacious leaders who do not tolerate a pirate mentality on their team.

Bodacious leaders believe in getting sustainable results by being extraordinary, unrestrained, and bold in their approach. They realize ordinary leaders can deliver short-term results; however, bodacious leaders strive to be extraordinary through steady, healthy, long-term growth. Bodacious leaders are unrestrained and see beyond the horizon, because they boldly go to the horizon and can see more than an ordinary leader. Bodacious leaders are in for the long haul and have a vision that extends beyond the next quarter or year-end.

Bodacious leadership goes beyond the pedigree and resume of the individual. Bodacious leadership demands people of wisdom, vision, integrity, and loyalty. Good people are assets to bodacious leaders and are not seen as an expense to reduce during lean times. Bodacious leaders keep their organizations lean by boldly reducing the number of pirates and underperforming team members. Their organizations are lean at the top and strong on the front line of business. People resources are massed closest to the customer, as opposed to the corporate office. Bodacious leaders build a strong customer focused structure that is lean at the top and focused on serving the customer.

Bodacious leaders understand good people and the customer are the primary means of realizing the organization's vision. They have a long-term vision and consistently get more out of their people by moving them toward the horizon and the ultimate destination. Bodacious leaders align their people resources with the vision of the organization and are willing to pay a short-term price for long-term gain. Bodacious leaders are different because in everything they do they strive to be extraordinary, unrestrained and bold.

BODACIOUS LEADERS
AND THE ARNOLD PRINCIPLE

Bodacious leaders are like Arnold the ranch owner who I worked for as a cowboy and told us, "…You may think I am in the cattle business; well I ain't, I am in the steak business. My business is to provide my customers with the best tasting and most tender steaks possible….To get tender steaks we must move the herd persistently and gently."

The Arnold Principle simply stated is, "Know what your destination is and clearly communicate how you are going to get there." Arnold understood the customer did not buy the whole cow; they bought tender steaks. Arnold had a long-term customer focused point of view that defined the way we did things on the ranch.

Bodacious leaders embrace "The Arnold Principle" by defining the way things are done in the organization to deliver a quality product to the customer. Bodacious leaders do not focus on the cow; they focus on delivering the best steaks to the customer. Bodacious leaders encourage innovation though persistence and by gently moving their teams toward the horizon.

Arnold did not have a pedigree or an impressive resume listing the universities he had attended, degrees obtained, or prior positions held. He did have a clear vision and understood his mission, which he effectively communicated to the team. While his vision and mission statements were not printed and distributed to all the cowboys, we understood the mission and understood we were in the steak business.

Embrace "The Arnold Principle" by clearly communicating your destination and mission. Avoid being tangled up with carefully crafted, corporate sounding vision statements that few people remember or understand. Keep it short and simple and communicate it regularly in plain understandable language.

BODACIOUS LEADERS ARE TEAM LEADERS

Arnold handpicked the cowboys who worked for him, and he had a long list to pick from because most cowboys wanted to work on his ranch. Cowboys aspired to work for Arnold because he was a man of integrity and he ran a good operation. Cowboys understood if they worked for Arnold and did a good job, their pay would be fair and they could depend on having work. Other ranch owners were interested in hiring cowboys when there was work and then letting them go when things slowed down. The best cowboys wanted to work for someone who had the ability and desire to keep them on during the lean times, as well as the good times. Arnold understood that if he wanted the best cowboys to work for him, then he had to look at the long-term and not short-term results. He invested in his cowboys, and the good ones returned his investment with commitment, loyalty, and hard work. Arnold believed that if he was going to provide the best steaks to his customers, then he needed the best cowboys who were committed, willing to work, would work as a team, and follow the direction of the leader.

When it came time to move the herd from the pasture to the main ranch, Arnold was diligent in communicating the plan and the final destination. Then he assigned team positions that included a cowboy riding point, a few cowboys riding flank, a cowboy bringing up the rear and someone to lasso the strays. All of the positions were essential to moving the herd. He identified every key position on the team and assigned someone to the role. Arnold understood he could not move the herd alone; he needed a team to guide the herd to the final destination.

Bodacious leaders understand that they cannot move their herd by themselves, so they build a committed team comprised of capable people who are willing to work and follow directions. Bodacious leaders are committed to growing people and encourage them to take on larger roles; by doing this they attract the best people who aspire to be part of the team.

People like to be on winning teams where they can also win individually. Leaders, who have a long-term vision and demonstrate integrity and wisdom will attract the best people and create a winning team. The best way to attract people, keep people, and ultimately win is through extraordinary, unrestrained, and bold leadership of a team.

BODACIOUS LEADERS KNOW THEIR HERD

A cowboy spends a lot of time with the herd and can identify the cows by their different markings, faces and personalities. You may be surprised to know that cows have different facial features and personalities, but in fact, they do. Some cows are leaders in the herd and others follow the herd, some are aggressive and others are more passive. Some of the cows are pretty (in a cow way) and others are just ugly.

A good cowboy becomes familiar with the individual cows by spending time with the herd. Cowboys do not spend time in meetings with the other cowboys and the ranch foreman discussing the cows and their needs. Cowboys go to where the cattle are and spend time among the herd.

Spending time with the team you lead is the best way to learn about each person. Arnold knew the abilities and uniqueness of each cowboy on the ranch because he spent time with them. Rarely did he saddle his horse and ride off in the pasture or drive away in his truck without a cowboy by his side. Arnold used his time with an individual cowboy to observe their work and to provide immediate coaching. Arnold did not spend much time in his small office, and "meetings" were actually coaching sessions that took place on the job during the course of work. Cowboys were comfortable sharing their ideas and opinions with Arnold because he would not belittle people or put down their ideas.

Like Arnold, Bodacious leaders know their people and embrace opportunities to get to know them better. Bodacious leaders have coaching sessions where people are talked with, instead of talked to. This approach creates an environment where individual contribution is encouraged and valued. The cowboys recognized and respected Arnold as the boss, not because he demanded it, but because he deserved and earned it.

Bodacious leaders have the unique ability to ride along side their people while leading them at the same time. The following is an example of the concept of riding along side, while leading:

Everyone on the ranch recognized Arnold as what we called, "the head honcho." Arnold established his leadership by spending time among the cowboys. He demonstrated that riding with the team does not mean the leader absolves himself from leading the team. By riding with the team, the leader understands the strengths and needs of the individuals and assigns tasks that best fit each individual. Arnold knew who was the best roper and would assign that cowboy to round up the strays. He also knew who was the best rider and would assign that cowboy to ride ahead of the herd. Because Arnold spent time with his cowboys, he knew the individual strengths and could put the right person in the right position.

Arnold also knew who was good enough and cared enough to be part of the team. Only cowboys who had the desire to contribute and the talent to perform with the best cowboys stayed on the team. Arnold told me one time, "There are cowboys who can and will, and then there are those who can't or won't. You cannot keep cowboys who cannot do it, or those who do not want to do it. So, quickly identify those who can and will, and those who can't or won't."

Arnold realized the best cowboys could not carry the dead weight of a cowboy who was unwilling or unable to perform at the highest levels. Being the Bodacious leader, he was, Arnold quickly replaced cowboys who could not or would not perform with someone who could and would do the job.

Sadly, organizations are bloated with ineffective leaders who spend most of their time in meetings and diagnosing the ills of team members, they rarely meet with and do not know. Ineffective leaders demonstrate managerial arrogance by prescribing solutions for teams they do know or respect. Conference calls, e-mails, and web conferences become substitutes for personal contact, and formal reviews, which occur once a year, take the place of one-on-one coaching.

Therefore, if you want to be an ineffective leader, just lock yourself in your office away from people and breathe your own air. Do this for awhile and you will grow in arrogance and conceit instead of gaining relationships and knowledge of your team. As results decrease and good people leave the organization, you can continue to sit behind your closed door and blame your people and the conditions that are out of your control. In the end, you are the leader, and your failure to lead will be evident in the results. There is a better way, the bodacious way. Open your door, get out of meetings, stop spending so much time with yourself, and spend time with your people.

BODACIOUS LEADERS PROTECT THE HERD

Part of a cowboy's job is protecting the herd from harm. Predators, such as the wolf, present a significant threat to small calves in the herd. Roaming under the cover of darkness, wolves travel in packs, looking for the opportunity to attack a newborn calf or a sick, weak cow. A single wolf alone is rarely a threat; however, a pack of wolves can overcome a protective mother and attack her small calf. Sometimes wolves become such a threat to the herd that the cowboy would need to take action, including eliminating the wolves in order to protect the herd.

Bodacious leaders protect their team and diligently look after their best interest. They insure that predators do not prey on members of the team. While you do not have to worry about wolves, there are predators that prey upon your team members. The predators you have to protect against are those individuals or groups who evaluate and offer unsolicited opinions about the shortcomings of your team or individual members. Predators are unqualified to offer evaluations and base their evaluations on a narrow knowledge based on an individual or team. Like wolves that hunt in packs and travel under the cover of darkness, predators do the most damage when they operate in packs and travel under the cover of a meeting environment. Predators use the cover of a meeting environment to offer unqualified evaluations of an individual or a team to senior management. The predators may offer their evaluation based on a single interaction or experience with an individual or a department.

Predators may single out a team member who did not respond to the request of a predator or predator's department as promptly as they wanted, or, your team member may not have executed a project or program that was important to the predator or predator's department. No matter the instance, a predator will base their unsolicited negative evaluation on a limited exposure to the person or team. Predators are takers; they want what they want when they want it, and if they do not get it their way, watch out, because the hungry predator will be on the prowl.

Bodacious leaders protect their team from predators by standing-up to predators, taking firm action, and defending the team member under attack. From this bold action, predators learn to respect the sovereignty of the bodacious leader's team.

For example, people in marketing, finance and other departments may become frustrated with a sales person or sales manager who does not execute a project deemed important to that specific department. In these situations, the sales manager has to take into account the full scope of what is being asked of the individual and determine if he or she was delivering on their primary mission, which is selling.

Bodacious leaders cannot allow team members to be evaluated by a single interaction with an individual or a department. Only the bodacious leader is qualified to evaluate an individual's performance based on the goals and objectives given to the person. As a manager of a sales organization, I discovered there were many people who would willingly give advice and guidance to salespeople on how to sell more. Unfortunately, many of those offering advice and designing programs for the sales team had never been in sales themselves.

On the other hand, just as many sales people or sales managers get in predator mode and believe they are qualified to evaluate individuals in other departments. Bodacious leaders do not tolerate team members that go into the predator mode and will act quickly stop the attack.

A Bodacious leader is capable of evaluating his or her people because they spend time with them. Bodacious leaders hold their teams to the highest standards of performance and integrity. They do not protect team members because they are good friends, attended the same school, or because they like them. They protect and defend team members who have high integrity and bring value to the organization. Bodacious leaders are careful not to defend their team or individuals if they have truly messed up. Under no circumstance will a bodacious leader defend an individual of low integrity. Bodacious leaders weed out team members of low integrity or those who bring no value. They understand that allowing a single person of low integrity to remain on the team taints the integrity of the entire team and the leader.

No matter what type of team you lead, as a bodacious leader you must protect your team from predators, members of low integrity, and those who bring no value. As long as your team is compromised of people of impeccable integrity, and the team is consistently held to the highest standards, then you can stand confident to defend them in any situation.

YOUR MOST IMPORTANT HERD

As a bodacious leader, you will have opportunities to lead or be a part of different teams. The more evident your bodacious leadership becomes to others, your opportunities to lead or participate will increase. Your opportunities will vary from leading people in business, to leading in volunteer organizations in your community. Just as a magnet draws iron, people are drawn to a bodacious leader, which allows opportunities to grow for everyone.

Leading teams can be likened to herding cattle, and at times it may seem easier to herd cattle than to move a team in the direction you want to go. By far the most important herd, and at times the most difficult herd you will lead may be your family. The family herd is unique with each member possessing their own personalities and values. It's amazing how children raised by the same parents can often be vastly different. One child may follow the instruction and direction of the parents, while another child in the same family may constantly stray from the herd and has to be lassoed back in. The family plays an important life-forming role for all members, and leading your family is the most important leadership role you will ever have.

Television has based many programs around different types of families. Your family may have been like "Leave it to Beaver" or it may have been more like the "Addams Family." Regardless of the family experience you had as a child, your job is to provide bodacious leadership for your family. How you lead, your family will play a major role in shaping the ideas and values of your children.

Your leadership role in the family may be as the father, mother or as stepparent. No matter the leadership role you play, your impact on the family is great. You cannot delegate the family leadership responsibility, hire it out, or pass it off. The role of leading the family falls squarely on the shoulders of the parents. The opportunity to lead a family comes only once and is over before you know it. Cherish your time as a parent, and do not trade the opportunity to lead your family for a career, hobby, activity, or money. Make leading your family the number one priority, and you will never regret your commitment to lead those who need you most. You can never regain lost time with your spouse and children. Someday the kids will be raised and gone; you cannot reach back and regain that lost time.

BODACIOUS LEADERSHIP REQUIRED

- Move your team gently
- Know what business you are in
- The Arnold Principle: Know your destination and clearly communicate how you are going to get there
- Get to know your team members by spending time with them
- Protect your team from predators
- Lead your most important herd: Your family

CHAPTER SIX

Rocket Fuel

ROCKET THE DOG

WHEN I WORKED ON THE RANCH I HAD A DOG named Rocket that was a loyal, rough looking mutt that had a lot more personality than looks. Simply put, Rocket was flat out ugly. However, as he lazily ambled toward you, his tail wagging and an odd-looking dog smile on his face, you could not help but warm up to him.

Rocket would eat anything, well almost; he did not like canned or packaged store bought dog food. No matter how good the brand or how fancy the label, Rocket preferred leftovers. Preferably, food you had slopped around in on your plate. Only when there were no leftovers, would Rocket begrudgingly eat store bought food.

Rocket really liked chicken bones and chocolate. Yeah, I know both of those kill dogs, the only thing was Rocket did not know that, and at the time neither did I. The way I looked at it, if he could drink from the toilet and eat dead frogs, then a few chicken bones and pieces of chocolate would not hurt him. To facilitate his diet, I would buy the no-name brand chocolate chips and toss them to him as a little dessert each evening. As for the chicken bones, he would eat any of them from the leg bone to the breastbones. Rocket was handy, you see, we did not have a garbage disposal, with him, we did not need one.

Catching chicken bones in mid-air was the closest thing to a trick that Rocket could perform, but he could nail that chicken bone mid-air with no problem. Rocket probably never really tasted the chicken bones, because he would devour the whole bone in one bite. One evening I was tossing chicken bones to Rocket, and he was doing his "trick."

Rocket was getting a little older, and did not jump quite as well as he did when he was a young pup. However, he still loved to catch chicken bones and wolf them down in one bite. Well on one fateful day, I tossed him a chicken bone a little too soon after he had just wolfed down the previous chicken bone. He jumped up and did a nice mid-air catch, but there was a problem. The chicken bone did not go down, it stuck in his throat with just a small amount sticking out of his mouth. Rocket began to gag and choke, and I could see he was in trouble. Not knowing what was required to modify the Heimlich maneuver to work on a dog, I just froze. Rocket was in real trouble, gasping for air he dropped to his doggy knees, and I knew I had to do something or Rocket would die. Reaching into his slobber-dripping mouth, I grabbed the chicken bone and pulled it from his throat. In a moment, Rocket caught his breath, revived his senses, and lunged toward me ripping the chicken bone out of my hand, almost taking off my little finger in the process. Then with slobber flying, he proceeded to wolf down the very chicken bone that almost killed him.

WHAT IS CHOKING YOU?

Rocket loved chicken bones and chocolate. Supposedly, chicken bones can splinter when the dog chews them and the splinters can stick in the dog's throat. I have recently become aware that chocolate is poisonous to dogs. If I had known these things were bad for dogs and posed a risk, I would have not fed Rocket chicken bones or chocolate. Rocket would not of been pleased, but he would not have been exposed to the risk that both presented.

It is one thing to continue doing something that is not good for you when you do not know any better. However, when you become aware that certain things are unwise, dangerous or unhealthy you should have more sense than an ugly dog and stop doing those harmful behaviors. For example, when we are young, we believe we are bulletproof and that only "old" people have health problems. We also believe that "bad things will not happen to us," or that we are somehow exempt from consequences. When we are young, old age seems light years away. Ignorance, youth, and arrogance can blind us to the truth that someday we will pay the price for poor choices.

The important lesson here is not complicated. When you become aware that something you are doing is bad for you, stop doing it. Take time daily to reflect on what you did the day before and consider the wise and unwise choices you made. Do not lie to yourself or rationalize the bad things you are doing. It is too easy for us to rationalize and continue doing things that are bad for us. It is always easier to keep doing the things that are bad for us than it is to take steps to correct our unwise behavior.

Avoid comparing what you are doing to what other people are doing. For example, you may want to get better control of your finances but your measuring stick for progress is how your friends spend their money, the car they drive, the house they live in, or the vacations they take. Your measuring stick for progress should not be gauging your bad habits to other people whom are in worse shape than you are. Strive to fulfill your own personal goals and not the goals set by the lifestyle of others.

CHOKING YET?

Under any other condition, it was very unwise for me to stick my fingers in Rocket's mouth; he had a tendency to eat whatever was placed in his mouth. However, when he was choking on the chicken bone he needed help, and he was willing to allow me to reach in and remove the chicken bone. Only when he was desperate and unable to help himself was he willing to accept help and not bite the hand that fed him.

Unfortunately, we continue to do unwise things because we enjoy them and refuse to help ourselves or allow others to help us. Too often we "bite the hand that feeds us" by making unwise choices and refusing wise council by trusted advisors. We are blinded at times and cannot see that the unwise activities and choices that are choking us. All of us at times need trusted advisors who can provide wise council and point out the chicken bones and chocolate dangers in our lives.

When I put my hand in Rocket's mouth to remove the chicken bone that was choking him, it required courage and I risked physical harm if he mistook my finger for a something else to eat. Trusted advisors are people of courage who are willing to risk harm to the relationship to help remove what is choking us. Sometimes we fail to acknowledge the things that are choking our effectiveness and personal growth because of pride. The Book of Proverbs of the Holy Bible warns us that "pride goes before a downfall." In most every instance, our pride blinds us to what is choking us and limiting us from experiencing total joy in our lives. Seek out wise counsel and listen to them when they point out what is "choking" you.

Marriages are destroyed, careers ended, friendships lost, good health compromised, and even lives are lost because some people fail to stop the "chicken bone and chocolate" activities in their lives. If we completely ignore wise council and continue bad behavior, we will choke.

The day will come when you need help; however, if you are not careful there may not be anyone there to help you. A "chicken bones and chocolate" lifestyle will choke out healthy relationships and alienate wise counselors who we should count on when we are blind and in trouble. Your opportunity is to heed wise council and make proactive changes in your life before you choke on your own pride.

Life can become so fast, hectic, and blurred by conflicting messages that you may be choking not even realize it. Some chicken bone and chocolate activities we are involved in are clouded as achievement, recognition, or enjoyment. Little by little, chicken bone and chocolate things can creep into our lives until, unknowingly, we poison and choke our relationships and effectiveness.

HOW TO FAIL BODACIOUSLY

From the first day I walked away from my job on the ranch and started working on the loading dock, I had dreams of climbing the ladder, having the corner office and achieving the great things in my career and my life. I now have the corner office, a job with a lot of perks, children with good marriages and several wonderful grandchildren.

The passion to live an extraordinary, unrestrained, and bold life has been my rocket fuel every since I walked away from the ranch. In pursuit of my bodacious dreams, I have made my share of mistakes and at times paid too high a price to achieve the wrong things. I have failed at more bodacious opportunities than I have succeeded at, but I learned from each success and failure. I discovered that along the way to realizing your bodacious life you will buck off more times than you ride the full eight, but the joy is truly in the ride. Just like in bull riding, there is no score and no chance to win from the bull you never rode.

There is no doubt I have got hung up on my share of chicken bone and chocolate things in my life, and I thank God for my wife Mattie who was quick to notice and guide me back to the pursuit of a bodacious life. Just remember we are all going to choke on chicken bones at one time or another; a quick recovery requires noticing and heeding advice of sound counsel around you.

You are also going to have some chocolate moments in life, those behaviors you love to do or participate in that are slowly killing you. Be quick to listen, be quick to change, and be persistent in your efforts to change your lifestyle and get back to living a bodacious life.

Along the way to pursuing my bodacious dreams, I worked too many hours, traveled too much, and should have spent more time with my family. There is little doubt that I would have done it differently, but I would have still done it. I do not regret that I made the bodacious ride and pursued my bodacious dreams. If you are waiting to pursue your bodacious dreams until you can do it perfectly without failure, then forget it; you are not ready to make the bodacious ride. Living bodaciously is not about living perfect, it is about living an extraordinary, unrestrained, and bold life. So strap on your spurs and get ready to ride, you are going to buck off, you're probably going to get run over a few times, people will laugh at you and discourage you, but get up off the ground and make another ride.

HELP FOR A CHOKING COWBOY

The spring breeze, scented by fields blooming with wild flowers blew gently over the Texas prairie. The sound of mourners singing the old hymn "Victory in Jesus" rang out over the cemetery as tears of sorrow and relief rolled down my cheeks. Standing near the casket of my father, I watched as his great-grandchildren placed freshly picked Texas wildflowers on his casket. For the first time in my life, I experienced opposite emotions simultaneously, great sorrow mixed with relief. There was sorrow over his death, knowing that I would miss him more than words could express, yet I was relieved that he would no longer endure suffering from the cancer that ravaged his aged, frail body.

Standing alone looking over the Texas prairie, I reflected on the legacy of my father and his impact on my life. Dad was an honest, hard-working man who did not amass great wealth or hold positions of great power. However, to me he lived a rich life and fulfilled his purpose. Dad was committed to his family and devoted to his Christian faith. Both Dad and Mom always taught the importance of faith, family, and work. My dad left me with good memories; sound teachings and was a role model for success in my work and family life.

Weakened by the treatments, Dad had little strength in his final days; even something as small as carrying on a conversion required great effort. Due to his weak condition, I spent my time at his bedside mostly just talking to him, bringing him up to speed on what was happening in the world and the lives of the family. Dad passed away before he had the opportunity to give me his final words of direction or wisdom.

There was a time in my life when the last thing I wanted from Dad was his advice or wisdom, but as he lie there, I saw my Dad as more than a father, he was a mentor and wise man. Even though Dad was unable to give me his final words from the life he lived, his words of encouragement and understanding are etched in my being. The morning following his passing, I rose early and wrote down the wisdom and teachings I learned from him.

I would say that my dad truly lived a bodacious life. To me he was an extraordinary man, unrestrained in his faith and bold in his courage. This should cause you to think about the impact you have every day on the people around you. What will your life reflect to the people closest to you? Live a bodacious life that reflects how you would like your final words of wisdom to be remembered.

Life is not about what you keep,
it is about what you give.

People remember your actions
more than your words.

Preach less and minister more.

Be gentle in suffering.

Be strong in suffering.

Be willing to sacrifice for others.

Submit to God and know He is with you.

Speak with kindness and gentleness.

Cherish the time you have with family.

Cherish the time you have to serve God.

Honor God, family and people.

THAT WAS THEN, THIS IS NOW

The evening following my dads' funeral I had a restless night. I had a lot on my mind and I tossed and turned most of the night, and after several hours, I finally dozed off in a restless sleep. My sleep was continually interrupted by the words, "That was Then, this is Now" running through my mind. I opened my eyes and looked at the clock, it was only 3:30 a.m. but I could not lie still a minute longer; I got out of bed and wrote down "That was Then, this is Now." I knew I had heard these before, but no matter, I was compelled to write them down. Quietly, I got out of bed so that I would not wake Mattie; I slipped into my closet and pulled on an old pair of jeans and a t-shirt. I worked my way through the dark house toward my office, as the phrase "That was Then, this is Now" ran through my mind. When I turned on the small lamp on the corner of my desk, I could see the picture of the five cowboys across my office on the bookshelf. I grabbed my pen I quickly wrote down, "That was Then, this is Now," on my notepad.

I sat back and looked at the picture of the five cowboys on my bookshelf. I wondered if one of them had used this phrase. Where had I heard it before? Maybe I read it in a book or heard it in a great speech. I know I had heard it before but just could not pin down the source. Then it came to me. It was not from some past experience. I heard it when I saw a car race on television earlier that afternoon. One of the announcers was talking about a driver who had not won a race in long time. As the driver lead the pack, the announcer used that phrase to describe the situation. I sat there awhile reflecting on the meaning of the phrase to my life.

I looked at the picture of the cowboys and me on my bookshelf; it brought back so many memories. It seemed that my work as a cowboy had occurred such a long time ago; so many things had changed from working on a cattle ranch to running a billion dollar organization. How did it happen? How could a cowboy without a college degree go from a ranch to a corner office? Then it struck me, "That was Then, this is Now" is how it happened.

The cowboy picture represented my "then," nothing could change the fact that I was cowboy, and I did not want to change it. It is the life you live beyond your "then" that makes the difference. Living in my "now" and pursuing my bodacious opportunities has allowed me to direct how my future and ultimately how my history will be written.

LIVING IN OUR "THEN" IS CHICKEN BONES AND CHOCOLATE

We cannot change our past; we can only change how we live today. Living in our chicken bones and chocolate past, or our "then," chokes and poisons our "now." Events of your "then" have a heavy influence on the way you think and act. If you continue to indulge yourself in your then you will not be able to focus on your now.

Bodacious living focuses on what you can change, instead of what you cannot change. You cannot allow the past to be the primary author of your future; what you do now makes the difference in your life. You cannot continue to focus on your deficiencies, past failures, lack of education, or how others have hurt you, so get over it and start living in your now. Continued focus on your then is like my dog Rocket who loved the chocolate that was poisoning him and the chicken bones that choked him. Continued focus on your then will poison and choke your progress and will keep you from pursuing your bodacious dreams.

Be smarter than a chicken bone-eating dog; decide to change what you can change. Be extraordinary in your now, unrestrained by your then and boldly pursue your dreams, so you can be Bodacious.

WHAT YOU PLANT TODAY DETERMINES YOUR HARVEST IN THE FUTURE

You cannot change your past; it is behind you and forever recorded as history. The picture of me with my four cowboy friends was evidence of my past, but did not have to be a predetermining factor of my future, unless I allowed it to be a factor. I was a cowboy then, but I am not a cowboy by vocation today. I choose to change my life's direction; if I had allowed my past to author my future, I would have only performed cowboy functions. I would have never dreamed of life beyond the ranch, much less having the corner office.

You live with the decisions and consequences of your past; this does not change. But your ability to deal with your past failures and to put them in the past directly impacts how you live today. The only way you can make meaning of your past is to focus on what you do today, because what you do today will be tomorrow's past. You write your own history and legacy by what you do today. If you want to change your history and future, change what you do in the present. Instead of reaching back, reach forward and write your own future.

To get the most out of everyday and every moment in the day requires extraordinary commitment, unrestrained action, and a bold dream. Your dream and the best planning will be worthless if you accept the ordinary, remain restrained by your past, and are too fearful to pursue your dreams. To realize your bodacious dream requires that you to step outside your comfort zone. Moving from ordinary to extraordinary requires work and commitment. At first removing your restraints will make you feel uncomfortable and becoming bold, instead of fearful, will require courage. However, by making an extraordinary commitment to your dream and by committing to being unrestrained in how you use your now, allows you to write your legacy. This is a universal truth.

On the farm if you plant corn you will grow and harvest corn. If you plant wheat, you will harvest wheat. It is ridiculous to think you could plant corn and harvest wheat; it simply does not work that way. The same principle applies in how you use your now; what you plant today will be your future harvest. So if you want to change your future, change what you are doing today. Plant bodacious dreams today and you will harvest bodacious opportunities in the future.

If I had decided to do nothing different in my now, and if I had not pursued my bodacious dreams, I would probably still be working as a cowboy or would have settled for another "chicken catching" job. The now event of quitting my ranch job was followed by another now event at the crossroad when I made a "right turn" and took the longer, more scenic route. I turned my truck around and I did something different in the moment. I asked about the sign that advertised, "Hiring Loading Dock Workers," which was another now event, which landed me the first job with the company that I now own. It all began with a bodacious dream that stirred me deep down and my decision to be extraordinary, unrestrained, and bold.

Remain focused on your bodacious dreams, and you can change your future. Have bodacious dreams, extraordinary commitment to your dreams, and take unrestrained action to realize your dreams. Act boldly. Plant bodacious seeds today and you will harvest bodacious opportunities in your future. Be Bodacious; escape your chicken catching, chicken bones, and chocolate life by having a bodacious dream and planting bodacious seeds today.

YOUR ROCKET FUEL

- Get the chicken bone and chocolate things out of your life
- Know what is choking you
- Don't be restrained by your past
- Have a Bodacious dream
- Change your future by changing what you do today

CHAPTER SEVEN

Give Bodaciously

 ROCKET WAS A LOYAL DOG, BUT HE WAS NOT particularly smart or pretty. Actually, he was nothing more than an ugly, dumb old dog that loved to eat things that were bad for him. He could have had store bought food if he wanted, but he was satisfied eating table leftovers that someone had slopped around in. Rocket had a choice, but he chose to eat leftovers. You also have a choice. You can choose to sit by the table and beg for leftovers resources and morsels of time, just play dumb and accept what you get, or you can have first choice of the best life has to offer.

It is your choice; you can choose leftovers and live life short on time, money, and relationships or you can serve yourself first. You have the choice of what you do with your time, your money, and the people you spend your time with. It is all right to serve yourself first and expect to get the best of what is available. While not everyone has the same amount of money, everyone does have the same amount of time. Time is the great equalizer for everyone, and you are no exception. No one has invented a machine or potion that can give you more time. Making the best use of your time is your responsibility. How you deliberately use your time and resources will put you on the path to living an extraordinary, unrestrained, and bold life.

Be Deliberate in Your Now

The word "deliberate" means to do something intentionally or on purpose, even if you do not feel like doing it. Being deliberate, intentional, and persistent will move you from begging for table scraps to enjoying the best of the two things you do control, your time and your resources (money).

How is it then, if you have control over your time and money that you feel there is never enough of either? Perhaps it may be, you are allowing others to take the best parts of your time and money first, and you are accepting the leftovers. The truth is, if you allow others to take your time and money and use it the way they choose to first, you will always feel out of time and out of money.

You can live on the leftovers, or you can take the best part first provided you live by the Four Principles of Deliberate Living listed below:

Four Principles of Deliberate Living

- Deliberately set aside time for yourself
- Deliberately set aside time for others
- Deliberately give money to others
- Deliberately save money for yourself

These four principles may sound selfish when you first read them. However, when you fully embrace these principles and live by them you will stop living on leftovers and start living a deliberate and bodacious life. Deliberately setting aside the first portion of your time and money is the key to the four principles.

DELIBERATELY SET ASIDE TIME FOR YOURSELF

Setting aside time for yourself may sound selfish; however, it is anything but selfish. Life can be hectic and schedules are demanding for everyone. As you grow your career and your family, it will seem there is just no time left for you. However, it is important that you set time aside for yourself where you think about your goals, evaluate your progress, work on your projects, dream your dreams, and pray your prayers.

Deliberately setting aside for yourself will have a huge impact on your personal growth and your happiness. Your life will feel less rushed and you will not finish the day feeling starved for just a little time for yourself. Consistent observance of time set aside for yourself allows you to feel less stressed, be more content, and provides you a greater degree of control over your life.

You may be thinking, "Sure setting aside time for me sounds great and I would love to this, but after everyone else has their share of my time there is none left over." Before you discount it as impossible, consider how you might be able to carve out thirty minutes or an hour each day. How could you rearrange your daily schedule to find time for yourself without robbing time from work or family? Finding time for yourself requires deliberate planning, extraordinary commitment, unrestrained action, and bold change to make it a reality.

How to Find TIme for Yourself

When I worked as a cowboy, I needed to work seven days a week to make enough money to support my young family. During the week, I would work my job on the ranch, and on the weekends, I would milk cows for dairy farmers who wanted to take a day off. Working on a dairy requires that the cows be milked twice a day, once in the early morning and once in the late afternoon. The early milking started at 4:00 a.m., so that meant I had to get out of bed at 3:00 a.m. to have time to get to the barn, bring the cows from the field to the barn, and get the equipment ready to go. When I first started milking cows, I hated getting out of bed at 3:00 a.m. However, the longer I milked the cows, the easier early morning hours became, and over time I was transformed into a morning person. After getting up early for several years to milk the cows, I noticed that at 4:00 a.m. there are not many people asking you to do things or imposing their agenda on you.

Years later when I no longer had to milk cows on the weekends to make ends meet, I still found myself getting out of bed early in the morning. The early morning hours are my time, when no one else is awake, the house is quite, the phones are not ringing and there are no e-mails to answer. In the early morning hours, I can have my thinking time, my dreaming time, my relaxation time, and my prayer time all without taking time out of my family time or work time. Trust me, at 4:00 a.m. no one wants to have anything to do with you; you are on your own.

The point of this is not to convince you to get out of bed at 4:00 a.m. for your personal time. What I want to point out is that you can find time for yourself; it just depends on your level of commitment. You may be a night person who has more energy in the evening and cannot bear the thought of getting out of bed one minute earlier, much less an hour earlier. If you are a night person, then find your time after everyone else is in bed. On the other hand, you may be a person who needs a full eight or more hours of sleep and taking an extra hour in the morning or evening simply will not work for you. Then look closely at your daytime schedule; you may have time during your lunch break or other times during the day.

What is important is that you find at least one hour a day that you set aside for yourself. It is important that you do not rob from your work or family time, but that you discover the one hour that you can set aside for yourself. Your personal time will not magically appear; you will have to be deliberate in setting it and must remain persistent in observing the time you set aside for yourself.

THE DAY STARTS WHEN YOU WANT IT TO START

It is important that you make your personal time the first thing you do every day. You may be wondering how you can do this if the time you set aside for yourself is in the evening or during your lunch hour? If you think about it, your personal day can begin when you decide it begins. The clock says a new day starts at 12:00 a.m. every day; however, most of us are not out of bed at this time of morning. Usually, you start your day when you get out of bed; but it does not have to start then. Declare when your day begins, it does not have to begin when you get out of bed it can start when you want it to start. Reset your personal 24-hour clock to begin when you want it to begin and make your personal time the first thing you do. Take control and decide when your day begins and ends; just make your day start with you.

If you are a morning person, then get up an hour earlier to observe your time. If you are a night person, stay up an hour later and start your day in the evening with your time. Making your personal day begin with your time is important because you are giving to yourself first; you are taking the first part of your day before anyone else has the opportunity to take it from you.

The real key to observing your personal time is deliberately setting aside an extra hour a day. It does not matter when it is, but you have to be deliberate in establishing when you will have your time. You may be thinking that you just cannot get up an hour earlier or stay up any later. While you believe having time for yourself would be nice, you just do not think you have time in the morning or evening. Well, think about converting some of your "chocolate time."

CHOCOLATE TIME CAN BE YOUR TIME

Remember the story about my dog Rocket? He loved to eat chocolate and did not know chocolate was bad for dogs; all he knew was that he liked it. So every day, Rocket would wolf down as much chocolate as I would give him to eat.

In your life, "chocolate time" is the time you waste doing things that are not good for you, but you continue doing them because you like to do them. Your chocolate time may be watching too much television, spending too much time surfing the web, too much time on hobbies, too much time shopping, or any other array of activities you can name. These small morsels of time you waste each day doing things you "enjoy" actually do nothing to grow you personally. This is the definition of chocolate time. In fact, most of the chocolate time in your life may be hurting you and hurting your relationships.

Look hard at how you spend your day, is there any chocolate time in your day? Could you cut out an hour of television or web surfing, shopping, or hobbies? If you are honest with yourself, you can find at least one hour of chocolate time each day that could be converted to time for yourself.

To set aside time for yourself, you must be deliberate in how you use your time. You cannot get more time, we are all allotted same

24 hours, but you can control how you use your time. You simply need to go on a time diet and cut the chocolate time out of your life. Reducing the amount of chocolate time in your day will free up time that you can spend thinking about your goals, evaluating your progress, working on your personal growth, dreaming your dreams, and praying your prayers. I guarantee you that there is no television show that will benefit you more than taking an hour a day for yourself. Make it part of your day and a part of who you are, and you will experience personal growth and satisfaction beyond what you thought was possible.

DELIBERATELY SET ASIDE TIME FOR OTHERS

After you have set aside time for yourself, be deliberate in setting aside time for others. You may find it is easier to set aside time for yourself than it is to set aside time for other people, but you will grow personally and the people close to you benefit when you set aside time to work on self-improvement and personal growth. If you want to experience a bodacious life, you need to go beyond time set aside for you, and deliberately give time to your family and community.

Years after I left the ranch and my four cowboy friends, I found myself fully involved in the daily rush of work; trying to make ends meet and raising a young family. It seemed like we were trying to keep up with everyone else, comparing our lives and what we had to what other people had. For example, we went tent camping for vacations while our friends went on hotel vacations with their families. Our small home in a nice neighborhood was comfortable, but it was not like everyone else's newer and bigger home. We had used cars, and while reliable, they were not the new cars everyone else had. We did not have a boat, but "everyone else" did. Our bank account by no stretch of the imagination could be considered fat, but everyone else seemed to have more money and investment accounts. We were doing okay, but it appeared to us that everyone else was doing much better. It seemed that as we moved up, everyone else simply moved ahead of us. Mattie and I were happy, but we had fallen into the trap of comparing what we had to what everyone else had.

I had a good sales year one year and was fortunate enough to be awarded an all expenses paid Caribbean cruise in recognition of my performance. Mattie and I were excited about the cruise, because we had never been on a nice vacation, "like everyone else." Once we were aboard the ship and living the cruising life we were awe struck; it was better than we dreamed. The ship was fantastic and the food was unbelievable. We were living a life on the cruise ship that we had never dreamed of living.

On the cruise ship, just like when I was at home, I got up early to enjoy a cup of coffee, the sunrise and to take advantage of personal time. On the third day of the cruise, I was on deck early enjoying my personal time and struck up a conversation with José, one of the deck hands doing painting and maintenance on the ship. I visited with José while he stroked a fresh coat of paint on the railing near the deck chair where I sat. During my conversation with José I found out, he was from little village in Mexico. Because of the dire economic conditions in his village, he had to leave his wife and children behind so he could find work and send money back to his family.

Tears came to José's eyes as he told me about how much he missed his wife and children, but José swelled with pride when he said, "My children have shoes and can go to the doctor when they are sick, so for me it is worth the sacrifice."

José took a brief pause, glanced over the edge of the boat, and said, "I just wish the doctors could find out what is wrong with my son Leon because he cannot walk or control his hands. The doctors recommend that we take him to a specialist in Mexico City or in the United States. Unfortunately it is beyond our means, but I pray daily that God will send a Miracle Worker for Leon, and someday he will walk and play with the other children."

José dipped his paintbrush in the white paint and continued his story, "I really should be grateful though, the other children in the village are very poor, do not have shoes, and many of them are ill or have even died because their parents could not pay for a doctor. The last night before I left the village to work on this ship, the people of the village gathered and prayed that someday a Miracle Worker would come to the village and heal the children. I do not know; maybe someday the Miracle Worker will come."

José reached in his pocket, took out a piece of paper and quickly wrote some information on the paper. Handing the piece of paper to me José smiled and said, "Señor, I hope someday you can visit my village, you would be welcome." Taking the paper from José's hand I wondered to myself, *How I should respond?* As a gesture of goodwill, I gave him my business card and wrote my home address on it. I handed José my card, I courteously replied, "José, if you are ever in Texas come see me. You would be welcome."

I did not see José the rest of the cruise, but I often thought about his story and his plea for a "Miracle Worker." On the trip back home, José's story started to work on me. I tried not to picture the small children he told me about, barefoot in the hot desert dirt, but my thoughts drifted often to his son Leon. It was hard to believe that there were sick and dying children all because there was no money for a doctor. It wrenched my gut to think how helpless the parents must feel seeing their sick children go without care.

After hearing José's story, I felt like the most selfish, self-centered person on the earth, because if I compared his village and myself to José, I was indeed a wealthy man who enjoyed the blessing of abundance. The things I took for granted, such as shoes and medical care for my children were considered abundance for other people.

THE MIRACLE WORKER

A few weeks after I returned home a curious looking envelope arrived in the mail. The letter was from José, thanking me for talking with him that morning; his closing line simply read, "Remember to pray for a Miracle Worker, my village and my son's healing."

During the cruise, I had shared my visit with José with Mattie and she encouraged me to do something for José, but I had conveniently ignored her advice. I folded the letter and placed it on my desk; I decided to take Mattie's advice and do something for José. I did not know what could be done, but I decided doing nothing would be turning a deaf ear and a blind eye to a desperate plea. Not knowing exactly where to start I decided to place a call to David, one of my cowboy friends in the picture, and invite him to lunch. Maybe if I shared this with David, together we could come up with something.

David and I met for lunch a couple of days later and I told him José's story. After I finished the story, David replied, "If you want to do something about this; if you want to help José, then I will be there to help you."

To make a long story a little shorter, things started moving after our lunch meeting, over the next several months, David and I met with community and church leaders, doctors, and nurses. We worked closely with local organizations to get donations of medical supplies, and we put together packages for mothers with newborns and packages with other personal items for the children and adults.

During the time we were doing the initial planning, I maintained regular communication with José who had completed his contract on the ship and returned to his village. There were a lot of details and logistical needs. To bring it all together, David and I arranged a site trip to José's village so we could see it with our own eyes before we sent a large group several hundred miles to the remote village.

Not only did I want to see the village for logistics planning, but I also wanted to make sure it really existed and that José was for real.

It required two long days of driving to reach the village from our town in Texas. Finally, our trucks came to a stop at the end of long dusty dirt road. As we stepped out of our truck onto the hot desert dirt, we saw poverty and need beyond what I had pictured in my mind. Surrounded by a crowd of small children who were serving as self-designated guides, David and I made our way to José's house. I saw José running down the road to meet us well before we made it to his home. He shook my hand and gave us each a long embrace. He said, "*Gracias Señor, gracias.*" The next day, José guided us as we surveyed the small village, met with the people, and assessed the needs. The logistics of bringing a group of volunteers into such a rough environment would be difficult. The needs in the village were enormous and clearly justified doing something more for the people.

On the long drive back home, I wondered how I had got myself into such a big project. I had never done anything like this, so what made me ever think that I was up to do something of this magnitude? All kinds of doubt went through my mind and I felt under equipped to take on this huge task. With no one else to turn to, I turned to God and prayed, "God, help me, give me wisdom, courage, and strength to take on this task. I am unable, but I know you are able. So take over God and equip me, and bring the people and resources to make this happen."

Back in our Texas town, the effort to recruit volunteers for medical teams, construction workers, logistics teams, and people to care for the small children while the adults saw the doctors was well underway. The most difficult part of the recruitment was locating doctors who could give of their time and were willing to work in a rugged environment. We spoke with several doctors who could not break away from their schedules. Other doctors were concerned they would not have significant impact on the patients without proper equipment or facilities. However, almost every doctor we spoke with had a deep concern for people and understood the need, but for various reasons they could not join us. When it appeared we had run out of doctors to talk to, we took a long shot and visited with Doctor James who was one of the premier heart surgeons in Austin, Texas.

After telling Doctor James about the need and pitching our proposal for him to lead a medical team on a trip to the Mexican village, he leaned forward in his chair and replied. "I would love to help you, but I don't know that I am qualified."

His statement astonished me, and I asked, "Dr. James, why do you believe you're not qualified? You are the best heart surgeon in Austin." Doctor James replied, "Well that would help if we were doing heart surgery, but you need someone who can do general medicine. I have not done that for years. I am not too sure how well I would do under conditions that do not provide me with the right equipment. I'm really concerned that I may not be able to help many patients given the conditions."

Trying my best to convince Doctor James without sounding argumentative I pressed on, "Doctor James, we have been to the village and seen several children with small medical needs whom have never been to a doctor, I also saw others like Leon who has a crippling disease. While you may not be able to do something for every one of them; if you only made a difference for one child, it would mean everything to that child, and would be well worth your time, even if only one child is healed."

After a pause and deep breath, Doctor James replied, "I have a successful practice, and I have been blessed beyond what I ever thought possible. Accepting your proposal will cause a lot of scheduling complications for me in my practice; but I think I can work it out, so you can count me in. This is something I have thought about doing for a long time; I just never had the opportunity or the courage. Thank you for giving me both."

After months of planning, fund raising, and recruiting, our caravan of sixty volunteers headed for the Mexican border and José's village. As we drove away from our Texas town with a crew of people willing to dedicate their personal time, money, and comfort. I thought to myself, perhaps José's Miracle Worker may be part of our team.

Inside the van was total silence as we bumped along the rough dirt roads that lead into the village. Every person in our van was stunned by the stark poverty and rugged environment. Small children ran barefoot alongside our caravan of vans and trucks loaded with people and equipment. There was not a dry eye in the van when we stopped atop the highest hill in the village that we chose for our base of operations on our earlier visit, everyone was deeply moved by the need.

Over the next five days, our construction team built a small multipurpose building that could be used as a church, clinic or community meeting place. Our care team worked with the small children making small crafts, singing songs and handing out personal care kits. The personal care kits had basic hygiene products such as toothbrushes, toothpaste, and soap. Each child received a bag that contained crayons, pencils, and other small educational items. Many of the children did not have pencils, had never had crayons, and most received their first toothbrush. It was hard to believe that there were children in this world who had never had something as simple as a toothbrush and toothpaste. However, standing before us were smiling children whom were grateful to have their first toothbrush.

By the second day, our medical team was settled in and working efficiently given the difficult conditions. Doctor James and his team had already treated close to a hundred people, and as word spread to surrounding villages, more and more people brought their sick to see the doctors. Shortly after the team began work on the second day, I saw José bringing his son Leon up the dusty dirt road in a pushcart toward our makeshift clinic.

Catching Doctor James' attention, I asked him, "I know you're busy with patients who have been waiting a long time to see you, but if you can, I would like you to look at the young man in the pushcart. It is José's son, the boy I told you about in your office."

I motioned to José and he brought Leon under the shade of the tent where Doctor James had set up his examination room. Leon was a frail boy, unable to walk and he shook with uncontrolled tremors in his hands and legs. Doctor James looked at Leon in the pushcart and then asked us to move him onto the examination table so he could get a better look at him.

After a few minutes of examination, Doctor James looked up and asked me, "Can you take one of the trucks and go to a pharmacy for me? I need some medication for Leon that may help him. I realize it is a long way back to the Texas border, but I need this medication."

I took the signed prescription from Doctor James, climbed in one of the trucks, and made the three-hour trip to the Texas border. I arrived back at the village just as the sun set on the horizon, Doctor James met me when I got out of the truck and instructed, "Show me the way to Leon's house. Let's give him his first dose of medicine; I would like to see if there is any improvement by morning."

The next morning as the sun broke over the horizon, Doctor James and I sat drinking our early morning coffee and talking about the logistics of the third day. In the early morning light, I could see two people walking up the hill toward our camp. One of them was walking with the aid of a crutch, while the other person provided assistance.

Turning to Doctor James I quipped, "Looks like you are going to have patients early this morning."

As the two got closer, I could not believe what I was seeing. To my surprise, it was José helping his son Leon, who was walking with the aid of a crutch. It seemed impossible that this frail boy whom yesterday could not control his arms or legs was now walking with the aid of his father and a single crutch".

Doctor James stood up and blurted out, "I'll be; it was epilepsy. It really was epilepsy. We can help him. We can make him better! That boy is going to be okay!"

José embraced Doctor James and sobbed as he said, "*Gracias* Doctor James, you are the Miracle Worker we prayed for. Thank you for coming; thank you for helping Leon."

This event changed Doctor James' life as well as Leon's life. Doctor James returned frequently to this small Mexican village to treat the people there. Overtime he recruited many more of his fellow doctors to join in the effort to help more people on both sides of the border.

You Can Be A Miracle Worker

Learn from this story; set-aside time for others in need, give of your time, your money, and your talents and you can be a miracle worker, too. However, it will not be easy to give time to others; you must be deliberate and set aside time daily for your family and community. Be careful not to trade family and community time for work time.

The pressure to perform and compete in the workplace can easily deceive us into believing that trading family and community time in for work time is the right thing to do. Whether you are pulling double shifts, working late at the office, or spending night after night on the road, stop and evaluate how you may be short-changing your family and community time.

Do not be deceived into thinking that if you work insanely long hours to get the next promotion, then you will have time to spend with your family or work in the community after that. If you are not able to set aside time for your family and community in your current position, it will not become easier after your next promotion. If you find yourself having trouble taking time for vacation to spend with your family, then do not expect it will magically appear when you get your next promotion.

If you do not have time to work in the community, be it your church, charities, civic organizations, or other volunteer activities, then you are short-changing yourself and the community. Be a giver of your time to non-paid activities such as your family and community, and maybe, just maybe you will be a miracle worker.

DELIBERATELY GIVE MONEY TO OTHERS AND YOURSELF

Working as a cowboy meant doing many different jobs on the ranch and most of the jobs involved dirty, hard work. Working as a cowboy was not about riding the range looking for cattle; in fact, that was a small part of the job. Most the time cowboy work involved shoveling and lifting heavy loads with dust blowing in our faces.

Big Jim, one of the older, long time cowboys on the ranch, approached my four cowboy friends and me one day. Big Jim was a short man with a big beer belly that hung over his belt; you could say he was not a poster child for healthy living.

I remember the time Big Jim bought a new pair of fancy dress boots that made him very proud. After wearing them only a few times, the top of the boot separated from the sole. Big Jim was furious that the expensive boots came apart so quickly, so he took them back to the store where he bought them. The store was good enough to give him another new pair of boots, and after a couple times of wearing the second pair, they too came apart. Big Jim was so upset that he went back to the store and demanded a refund. The owner of the store examined the boots, and then he looked at Big Jim's feet, measured his feet, and then looked at Big Jim. After a pause, the storeowner advised Big Jim, "Sir, I will give you your money back; however, I cannot sell you another pair because there is nothing wrong with the boots. The problem is your feet are too small to support your weight. Our boots are not designed to withstand that much pressure." I still remember how Big Jim ranted about the storeowner telling him that he was too fat for his feet. Even though Big Jim refused to believe it, with just one look at him you could agree that the storeowner was right on target with his assessment.

One day after work Big Jim, asked us to go with him to visit his wife in the hospital. All the way to the hospital, Big Jim talked about how much he loved his wife, how she meant everything to him and he would get misty eyed as he spoke. At the hospital, Big Jim stood near the side of his wife's bed, telling her how much he loved her, missed her and prayed she would get better. After spending an hour or two at the hospital, Big Jim told his wife we needed to go, and he promised to be back the next evening to visit again.

During Big Jim's display of concern and love for his wife, I thought to myself, "Big Jim must really be a decent man." As we walked from the hospital room and down the hall, Big Jim wiped the tears from his eyes and exclaimed, "Well, my crying or worrying ain't going to make her get any better, so let's go drink some beer, do a little honky-tonking, and chase some women."

I could not believe what I was hearing. Just minutes ago, he was crying and telling his wife how much he loved her, and now he wanted to go honky-tonking and chase women. We spent the rest of the evening at Chip in Dance Land, one of the roughest honky-tonks around. My cowboy friends and I mostly played pool and drank a few beers, but true to his word, Big Jim danced and danced with every woman he could find in the place.

A few days later, Big Jim offered us the opportunity to haul hay for him at night after we finished our work on the ranch. He indicated there was plenty of work, and he would pay us five cents a bale and promised to have us back home every night by 11:00 p.m. so we could get enough rest to work on the ranch the next day. To five gullible young cowboys this sounded like a pretty good deal, we could make extra money after hours, and five cents a bale was double what most people would pay for hay haulers.

Hauling hay was perhaps the hardest work I ever did as a cowboy. Hay hauling involved loading hundreds of seventy-pound hay bales onto a flatbed truck and then moving them into a barn for storage. One person would drive the truck; another would pick the bales up off the ground and throw them on the truck while the other two stacked the hay bales on the truck bed. Hay hauling was hard hot work that required a lot of backbreaking labor.

Big Jim had us hauling hay at night, and that was nice because it was much cooler. We also got plenty of rest driving from the hay field to the barn, because it was a number of miles to the barn where we carried all the hay. I must admit, it did seem a little strange that we took hay from various fields and carried it to one barn such a long distance from the fields, but Big Jim told us the owner needed a lot of hay and he had to buy it from many different farmers. The story sounded good to us, and what did we care? We were making five cents a bale, which Big Jim promised to pay us at the end of the week so the details did not really matter to us.

On the third night that we hauled hay for Big Jim, we loaded our flatbed truck with hay, and made our way from the hay field to the highway. As we approached the hay field gate, a bright spot light shined on our truck from the highway. Big Jim stopped the flatbed truck about two hundred yards from the hay field gate and began his confession.

"Boys, I may have not told you all the details about our hay haul-ing. Actually, for the past couple of nights we have been stealing hay from this field. I reckon that is the police, so you boys might want to get the heck out of here. I will take care of the truck and hay."

We could not believe what we were hearing! Stealing hay, we did not know we were stealing hay! Big Jim had deceived us into help-ing him steal, and we were too stupid to realize what was going on. All five us jumped from the truck and ran across the pitch-dark hay-field. Big Jim revved the truck engine and took off in the other direction full speed across the dark field with the headlights off. We could hear the truck banging and clanging as Big Jim ran it across the rough hayfield and gullies.

We were not worried about Big Jim at this point; we did not care if the police caught him, because he deserved it. However, we were scared to death and did not want to be arrested for stealing hay, when we had no idea that we were stealing. We ran as far as we could, stum-bling along through the dark night until we finally came to a line of trees along a creek that provided cover from the spotlight that con-tinued to search across the field. Exhausted, we huddled in the brush to catch our breath so we could continue our escape and make our way back home. Under the cover of the creek bed and brush, we made our way out of range of the spotlight, crossed a fence line and began our long walk back home. The five of us walked for hours in the dark of night, across fields and through woods.

About daybreak, we arrived at the ranch where we worked. As we moved toward the ranch headquarters, I could not believe what I was seeing in the early morning light. Sitting in front of the small house that Big Jim rented from the ranch owner was the flatbed truck that Big Jim used for his getaway. There were a few bales of hay stacked on the truck; the rest of the hay must have fallen off during his wild escape. The truck fenders were dented, the front bumper was torn off, and overall the truck was a wreck. Unbelievably

Big Jim had managed to escape the police and get back to his house without being caught. As it turned out Big Jim had been in bed sound asleep for several hours by the time we got back to the ranch after our all night walk.

TAKERS

Big Jim was a taker. He took from his wife, his friends, and those he did not know in an attempt to get more for himself. My encounter with Big Jim, while unpleasant taught me that I did not want to be like Big Jim. I did not want to be a taker; I wanted to be a giver. While Big Jim was an extreme example of a taker, we can become like Big Jim in a less obvious way if we are not careful. Big Jim was driven by selfishness and greed. All of us, no matter who we are, have a bent toward being selfish and greedy.

My dog Rocket was a good and loyal dog, but he was a taker. Rocket lived to consume food, and if another dog was near when he got his food Rocket would wolf down every bit of his food quickly to prevent the other dog from getting even a single bite. If the other dog even attempted to get close to his food, Rocket would curl up his upper lip, show his scraggly teeth, and growl viciously.

Rocket was a taker and consumer; he was not a giver when it came to his stuff. Rocket and Big Jim had a chicken catching men-tality in that they believed there was not enough food or stuff to go around and certainly not enough to share. Even though I fed Rocket regularly and made sure he had plenty to eat, his mindset was that there was not enough to share.

Big Jim and Rocket both thought they had to get more than their share because there was not enough to go around. After observing Big Jim and Rocket and their chicken catching/taker mentality, I decided to have a chicken eater/giver mentality and embrace the philosophy of abundance instead of a scarcity.

You have a choice, you can go through life believing there is not enough to go around, or you can believe you have abundance. You can be a taker, or you can be giver. Being a taker is easy because it is your natural programming; it requires deliberate effort to go from being a taker to becoming a giver. There are plenty of takers in the world; you can choose to be an extraordinary, unrestrained, and bold giver, the choice is yours to make.

GIVERS

In contrast to Big Jim and Rocket, was Charlie, whom my cowboy friends and I worked for cutting grain one season. We liked Charlie so much we stayed on working at his place even though the work we did was a little harder. Charlie modeled giving by the way he lived his life. Charlie was a successful cattleman, farmer, and did very well in the land business buying and selling large pieces of property. He was a wealthy man with a large home that set atop a high hill overlooking the town. Charlie was a man who contributed to the local community and gave charitably to people in need.

Every Friday afternoon, we would go to Charlie's house and pick up our paychecks. One time, Charlie politely invited us into his home and offered us a chair in his office while he prepared our checks. He apologized for not having the checks ready that week and explained he got in from town later than he thought he would. While Charlie was writing our checks, I could not help but notice a handwritten note lying on the corner of his desk. While I knew it was not right to read the note without his permission, the first line caught my attention and drew me into reading the entire note that read as follows:

Charlie,

Thank you for your contribution of $100,000 to our new church sponsored children's home. Your generosity and sacrifice will make a huge difference in the lives of our young people and community. As agreed, you can rest assured your gift will be held in confidence.

Sincerely,

Pastor Ed

While I felt I had violated Charlie's privacy by reading the note, I am glad I did, because it made a big difference in how I viewed giving from that point forward. In the days that followed, I thought often about the note and was amazed that someone actually had $100,000, because that seemed like an enormous amount of money to me. However, what amazed me even more is that Charlie had given it away! *How could anyone give away $100,000?* I asked myself repeatedly? I thought Charlie was either much wealthier than I had thought, a little crazy, or maybe both.

One day Charlie invited me to go with him to town and help him load some feed for the new calves. I was excited about going to town with Charlie, and this was the first time he had invited me. On our way to the feed store we passed by the construction site where the church was building the new children's home. While I knew I should not ask, I just could not help myself, I had to know why someone would give away such a large amount of money. I worked up my courage and I blurted out, "Charlie, why did you give so much money to build the children's home?" The words no more left my lips that I began wondering how I could be so stupid.

Without saying a word, Charlie slowed his truck and stopped in front of the children's home. Charlie said to me, "Son, get out of the truck. I want to show you something." We got out of the truck and I followed Charlie across the construction site and down the street until he stopped in front of an old run down house overgrown with weeds and brush. Pointing to the house Charlie told me, "See that old house; that's where I grew up. I never knew my real parents. I lived there in that house with a loving couple who took me in. At first, they were very poor and it was difficult for them to take care of me, but they sacrificed so I would have some place to grow up. To me, they were Mom and Dad. I loved them because they gave up a lot to raise me. They have been gone for a few years now, but the principles they taught me about giving stayed with me.

Dad always told me, give when you have little and you will be entrusted with more. That is exactly what they did; they always took the first 10% of what they earned and gave it to the church. Then he would take the next 10% and put it in the bank. Mom and Dad went beyond 10% and gave even more to people in need and to the community. During the time I grew up, we did not have a lot of money, but nonetheless Dad always gave. He never expected anything in return and always felt it was a joy to give.

Dad always told me, "Charlie you determine how you will use your money, so remember to give no less than 10% to others through your church or charities, then save no less than 10% for yourself and then live on the rest. Beyond that strive to give big to others, make giving 10% the minimum. The more you give, I believe the more you will be entrusted with and the happier you will be. It is not about what you keep and what you spend on yourself. You will receive more satisfaction and long lasting benefit by giving charitably."

"I want to apologize for reading the note on your desk the other day; it just caught my eye and I read it," I said sheepishly when Charlie finished his story.

"Well, I have had people do worse things to me." Charlie said with a grin on his face, and then he continued telling his story. "No doubt you should not read stuff on people's desk, but I guess it gave me the opportunity to share this with you. The $100,000 that I was able to give to the children's home is the realization of a dream that my dad always had. He was giver and always talked about writing a check for $100,000 and giving it to a worthy cause. Well, my dad passed away before he realized his dream, but I carried on his dream and was finally able to write the check for this children's home project. In a way, Dad did realize his dream through me and through the principles, he taught me."

BE A BODACIOUS GIVER

That day I spent with Charlie made a big impression on me and formed my thinking about how to use my money. So much so, that for the first time that Sunday I gave $15 dollars to the church and opened my first savings account with a $15 deposit. For years after I thought about Charlie, giving $100,000 to the children's home and it always struck me as something that Charlie could do, but would most likely be well out of my reach.

The trip I made to José's village where I saw firsthand how people helped, and how Dr. James healed José's son of epilepsy, inspired me. Following that trip, I decided to take my giving to a new level and go beyond just giving of my time; I decided to carry on the $100,000 dream that Charlie passed on to me. At that time, I was not making a big salary and was raising two kids, so even the thought of giving away $100,000 seemed impossible. Nonetheless, I made it my goal and my dream that someday, somehow I would have the ability and the courage to write a check for $100,000.

Years passed by and I thought and prayed often about giving $100,000. I wondered that even if I had that much money some day, would I have enough courage to write the check. Having no idea where the money would come from or no idea if I was courageous enough to do it still inspired me. I believe it was this motivation to give that pushed me to pursue bodacious opportunities, look beyond my personal horizon, and achieve more than I ever dreamed possible. When it was not all about my abilities, my limitations or profiting, or just me, I became more courageous in pursuing new opportunities. I knew that if I wanted to give away $100,000 as Charlie had, that I would have to earn a lot of money. I was inspired to make more money for reasons that were different from simply wanting to grow my personal bank account and buy more stuff. I discovered that pursuing bodacious giving led to success and income needed to give great amounts.

So, have a bodacious giving goal and your income will follow in proportion. The more you strive to give, the more you will earn. I believe the bodacious giving principle will motivate and enable you to achieve your maximum income potential. Stop focusing on just yourself, and focus on giving more to others, by doing this you will find personal satisfaction that far exceeds having the biggest house, nicest car, or latest gadgets.

Being a bodacious giver begins with your commitment to live by the Four Principles of Deliberate Living:

THE FOUR PRINCIPLES
OF DELIBERATE LIVING

- Deliberately set aside time for yourself
- Deliberately set aside time for others
- Deliberately give money to others first
- Deliberately save money for yourself

Stop living on leftovers, and start giving to yourself and others the first portion of your time and money. Be extraordinary, unrestrained, and bold in your giving and your living!

CHAPTER EIGHT

Bodacious Adventure

MATTIE AND I CELEBRATED OUR TWENTY-FIFTH anniversary by taking a Caribbean cruise. During our cruise, we visited the beautiful island of St. Lucia where we enjoyed a land and water tour of the island. The land part of the tour offered great sightseeing as we drove on mountainous roads that twisted along the coast and through the rain forest. During the land trip, we walked into the crater of a sulfur-spewing volcano, explored a rain forest and toured small villages on the coast. On the water portion of the trip, we boarded a large sailing catamaran that took us on a tour of several bays and beaches on our way back to the ship.

During the sailing trip the catamaran took us to Marigot Bay, a perfect palm tree lined bay with towering mountains on each side. Entering Marigot Bay was like stepping into the pages of a travel magazine, the setting was perfect and exactly what you imagine the perfect hidden Caribbean bay to look like. As our catamaran moved slowly through the bay, Mattie pointed out the sailing yachts at anchor in the bay. On board the yachts, people were relaxing on the deck and enjoying the perfect setting of the bay. Mattie waved to the people aboard one of the yachts and made the simple statement, "It would be so nice to be sitting on a yacht in a beautiful bay like this."

That evening as the ship sailed from St. Lucia, Mattie and I sat on the back on the cruise ship, watching the sunset over the islands. While we sailed across the gently rolling ocean, I said to Mattie, "We are going to do that."

Puzzled, Mattie looked at me and asked, "Do what?"

"Sail a yacht in the Caribbean. Someday, we will sail into a bay like we saw today, and we will be sitting on the deck of a yacht."

Mattie looked at me and replied, "I think it would be great to sail a yacht in the Caribbean."

I was not sure if she gave me a positive response to encourage me or to get me to be quiet about it. Mattie probably thought it was just my thoughts coming out of my mouth before I considered what I was saying and most likely did not give my comment additional thought.

WHY NOT ME?

Early the next morning, I got out of bed and found a good place on the deck to enjoy a cup of coffee and watch the ocean move by in the pre-dawn light. As I comfortably sat in a deck chair, I spotted a yacht sailing near one of the distant islands. I thought how nice it would be to sail from island to island, dropping anchor along beautiful beaches or in secluded bays. Even though I had never sailed, or been on a sailboat other than a daytrip catamaran, I still thought it would be a great adventure.

I leaned back in my chair and watched the yacht sailing on the horizon and asked myself, "Why not me? If the people we saw in the bay can sail their yachts, why can't I?"

Looking at the yachts silhouetted against the early morning sunrise, spurred my dream on and caused me to think that perhaps this was a bodacious opportunity I should check out. I snickered to myself, because I had to admit that considering a yacht was a far departure from my chicken catching beginnings or working as a cowboy. It had been so many years since I worked as a cowboy, but it was still fresh in my mind and remained as part of my identity and part of my DNA. Going from a cowboy to a yacht captain are not things that really align, but neither did an ex-cowboy sitting on the deck of a luxury cruise liner exactly align. It is amazing how pursuing a few bodacious dreams can change your life so dramatically.

There are hosts of people who will discourage you from pursuing your bodacious dreams. You will encounter people who will tell you that you do not have the education, the experience, or the background. Do not let these people discourage you, move forward and pursue your bodacious dreams. If a chicken catching cowboy can go from the ranch to his dream of the corner office, you too can realize your dreams.

Ask "Why not me?" Then, stand firm, pay the entry fee, and take the bodacious ride. A cowboy knows if he is afraid to ride a bad bull, then there is no score and no chance to win the prize. This goes for you, too. You must pursue your bodacious dreams in order to win.

Remember my path as a bodacious dreamer; I went from being a cowboy to owning a large company. Once I saw what I could accomplish when I pursued my bodacious dreams, I expanded my dreams and even considered sailing a yacht in the Caribbean by asking, "Why not me?

THE EXTRAORDINARY, UNRESTRAINED, AND BOLD YOU

Do not exclude yourself from pursuing your bodacious opportunity because it may not fit who you perceive yourself to be. You will tend to frame who you are based on who you were and your past experiences. Instead of framing yourself on your past, look to the person you can become. In reality, you cannot change who you were in the past. Your opportunity to build your future is based on your bodacious dreams and the person you want to become. My past framed me as a cowboy, and I could have allowed my past to control all other opportunities in my life. The natural path for me would have been to pursue opportunities that fit the template of my cowboy past. While I am proud of my cowboy heritage and value the experiences during this time of my life, my bodacious dreams required me to be extraordinary, unrestrained, and bold and move beyond my scripted past.

In the small town Mattie and I grew up in, most kids did not have bodacious dreams, nor were bodacious dreams encouraged. As a kid I do not remember my family having any friends who were college educated or who held an executive position. People in our world had ordinary dreams of completing high school, getting a job, and having babies. While these were not bad dreams to have, they were not bodacious dreams. Pursuing ordinary dreams would not lead to the extraordinary, unrestrained, and bold life I desired.

The natural path would have been to only dream about my bodacious dream, continue my work as cowboy, and provide a living for our family. My exposure to the world beyond being a cowboy was limited. I had little knowledge about other career options, or continuing my education. I was generally ignorant of opportunities beyond that of being a cowboy, but thankfully, I did not let my ignorance stop me from asking, "Why not me?"

Do not let your lack of knowledge of things stop you from exploring beyond where you are today. Ask the following Why Questions:

- "Why not me?"
- "Why shouldn't I pursue my bodacious dream?"
- "Why shouldn't I do something other than what I am doing today?"
- "Why can't I be extraordinary, unrestrained and bold?"

Regardless of your background, your tendency might be to put too much weight on your past and allow it to shape who you are today and who you will become. Your heritage is part of your identity; you can take pride or regret your heritage, but it is still your heritage. You do not want to divorce yourself from your heritage; rather you should see it as your uniqueness. Embrace the opportunity to harness your uniqueness and use it to realize your bodacious dreams. To have a bodacious dream, begins by leveraging your uniqueness and breaking the restraints of our past scripting. You are the author of your future script, start writing it today.

THE HORIZON

Our cruise ship passed close to a large spectacular island with towering mountain peaks. However, I had no idea what the name of the island was; it would help if the islands had big signs so you could identify them. As we neared the main harbor of the island, I counted at least thirty yachts under sail. The sight of so many yachts fueled my dream of sailing and prompted me to think about how I could realize my dream.

I knew absolutely nothing about boats or sailing and assumed it probably cost a lot of money to own a yacht. The yachts looked expensive, and I didn't have that kind of money. Dreaming of sailing a yacht in the Caribbean was fun to think about, but the money would be a real obstacle to overcome. I leaned back in my deck chair and allowed myself to feel discouraged and frustrated that I might not have the knowledge or the money to realize my latest dream.

Here I was sitting on the deck of a luxury cruise ship, enjoying a life that twenty-five years ago Mattie and I would have not dreamed possible. Instead of figuring out an answer, I was feeling sorry for myself and scripting my reason for not pursuing my bodacious dream to sail a yacht. The script I was writing really had nothing to do with money or knowledge; it was because I was too lazy, satisfied with ordinary, and restrained by fear. This prevented me from looking beyond where I was today.

When Mattie and I were first married, I worked as a cowboy and we struggled to stretch the small paycheck to the end of each week. It always seemed there was a lot more week than there was paycheck. At that time, it was a big splurge for us to walk to the Dairy Queen for a hamburger and fries. Yet here we were enjoying gourmet meals and around the clock food on the cruise ship. Back when Mattie and I struggled to afford a hamburger and fries, it was beyond my horizon for us to dream that someday we could afford a Caribbean cruise, yet sure enough, we were.

Looking out over the ocean's horizon, I realized that I was not stretching to look beyond my personal horizon. I was not looking for answers; instead, I was making excuses based on who I was at that time. Ordinary, restrained, and fearful thinking partnered with my lack of motivation to go beyond my horizon doused my flames of enthusiasm.

BEYOND THE HORIZON

I got out of the deck chair and walked over to the ship's rail to get a closer view of one of the yachts sailing close to us. The brisk ocean breeze filled the sails of the yacht, causing it to lean over as it crashed through the rolling waves. Aboard the yacht, I could see only two people, a woman who was helping pull the lines and a man in a straw cowboy hat at the helm. The yacht proudly displayed the United States flag aft and unbelievably, a Texas flag from the forward spreader.

Unaware Mattie had joined me on the deck; I was startled when she asked, "Honey, what are you looking at?"

I pointed at the yacht and said, "Look at that yacht, they are flying a Texas flag and the man at the helm is wearing a cowboy hat. That could be us someday."

Mattie put her arm around my shoulder and replied, "I did not think you would forget about sailing a yacht and figured you would find some way to try to get me on board with your dream. If you want to do it, then let's do it, I will sail with you."

I was not too sure who was craziest, me for thinking I could sail a yacht or Mattie for being willing to sail with me. No matter that neither one of us knew a thing about sailing and had no idea where we would get the money, we decided that together we would go to our horizon and pursue the dream that lay beyond. We stood at the ship's rail and talked about sailing a yacht. Together we decided that when we returned home, we would go to as far as we could see and then we would be able to see farther. As far as we could see at the time, sailing a yacht in the Caribbean seemed to be a bodacious dream. However, I pledged to Mattie that I would research sailing and yachts and find out more.

After returning home from our Caribbean cruise, I began to research everything I could find about sailing a yacht in the Caribbean. To my surprise, I found a large number of websites, books and even monthly magazines dedicated to sailing yachts and cruising in the Caribbean. Through my research, I discovered we could sign up for classes and learn to sail at various levels of certification. The classes started with the basics of sailing, such as learning coastal cruising, open water cruising, and even how to sail across the Atlantic Ocean. None of the classes required that we own a yacht, because the cost of the course included a yacht to sail. In addition, I discovered, there was a sailing school located in Texas on Galveston bay. If we were committed to pursuing the dream of sailing a yacht, learning how to do it was readily available to us.

As I continued to research our dream, I discovered that we would not need to purchase an expensive yacht even after we took lessons. To my surprise, I found that there were hundreds of yachts available for rent all over the world. The yachts available for rent ranged from simple thirty-two foot sail boats to fifty-foot and larger luxury yachts. We could take our choice of well-maintained older yachts to brand new yachts with a wide selection of configurations and equipment selections. Moreover, we could rent the yacht of our choice for a day, week or month in exotic locations like the Caribbean, Mediterranean, and South Pacific, and even on Galveston Bay in Texas. I could not believe all the selections of yachts available at reasonable cost, especially when compared to owning and maintaining a yacht.

While on our cruise, I was prepared to put away our bodacious dream of sailing, because I thought we could not learn how or could not afford to do it. When Mattie and I agreed we would go to our horizon so we could see a little further, we discovered answers and solutions that were just beyond the horizon of what we could see. Be extraordinary, unrestrained and bold; go to your horizon, go to the edge of what you can see today and you will discover the answers just over your horizon.

COWBOY, SAILOR
OR COWBOY SAILOR

You may be wondering if a cowboy can sail a yacht in the Caribbean. Consider this, both Mattie and I now hold three sailing certifications and with our credentials; we are qualified to charter yachts anywhere in the world. We have sailed extensively throughout the Caribbean on numerous yachts ranging from 33' up to 54' luxury yachts. Over the past few years, we have spent at least thirty days a year under sail and have sailed hundreds of miles in the Caribbean without a hired captain or crew. We have anchored in some of the most beautiful locations in the world where we have explored sugar white beaches and exotic tropical islands. We have spent countless nights anchored in deserted bays under the light of a full moon. We have been able to invite family and friends to join us on our enjoyable sailing adventures to destinations they never dreamed they would ever go.

To top it off, we have been able to sail to all these destinations without spending hundreds of thousands of dollars to purchase a yacht. All the yachts we have rented were in new or nearly new condition, and the total cost for all rent is far less than what an initial down payment on a single yacht would have cost us.

EXPLORE BEYOND YOUR HORIZON

I share this story with you, not to promote sailing, but to make important points about bodacious dreams. Your bodacious dreams are yours to pursue, but it is up to you to pursue them. If you ever want your dreams to become reality, you must take extraordinary, unrestrained, and bold steps to pursue them.

By learning to sail for extended periods and navigate unknown waters, Mattie and I learned much more than a new recreational hobby, our sailing experiences have had profound impact on my personal, business, and even my spiritual life. Sailing a yacht in the Caribbean has inspired in me a new spirit of confidence, courage and a sense of adventure to go beyond my personal horizons. Instead of only looking at the horizon and dreaming about what lies beyond, I am inclined to go to my horizon so I can see further.

My dream of sailing a yacht in the Caribbean originated from a few inspiring words from Mattie. However, to realize the dream required a commitment of time and work, which in the end returned great dividends of learning and joy for Mattie and me. If a cowboy can go from the ranch to the deck of a luxury cruise ship and to sailing a yacht, then you can pursue your bodacious dreams just beyond your horizon.

Pursue Adventure

Dreaming about sailing across the ocean to the islands on the horizon sparked an adventurous spirit in me, although I never thought of myself as an adventurous person. Pursuing the adventure of sailing a yacht caused me to stretch beyond my self-imposed boundaries, pushed me out of my comfort zone and moved me to new personal horizons of accomplishments. Pursuing new adventures will fuel your spirit, which is important for your personal growth.

Have the courage to go to the edge of your known abilities, doing so will cause you to grow and learn new skills. Do not eliminate yourself from pursuing new adventures because of fear or laziness. Pursuing your new adventures will require extraordinary courage, unrestrained action, and boldness. The only way you can sail into new harbors of your life is to have the courage to step out and take on new adventures. You make your own choices. You can choose to only dream about sitting on a yacht at anchor in a beautiful palm fringed bay, or you can take action and pursue your bodacious adventure. What is your bodacious adventure? Dream bodacious dreams and pursue bodacious adventures and you will live a bodacious life.

GET OFF YOUR BUT

Get serious about pursuing your bodacious dream, get off your "but," and do something. Be cautious of getting comfortable and resting on your big but, because your but will prevent you from pursuing your bodacious dreams. Buts come in many forms; here are a few that may look familiar to you:

* I would pursue my bodacious adventure but…
* I could have pursued my bodacious adventure but…
* But I did not know how to pursue my bodacious adventure…
* But I have never pursued an adventure like this before…
* But the bodacious adventure is too expensive…
* But pursuing the bodacious adventure will take too long…
* But what would people think if I pursue my bodacious adventure….
* But what if I fail at my bodacious adventure…

Your big but is the number one thing that is preventing you from pursuing your bodacious adventures. People with big buts rest on them and do not pursue bodacious adventures, you can be different; you can be bodacious. Get off your big but, take action, and make your bodacious adventure become reality.

My bodacious dream of sailing a yacht in the Caribbean would have never been realized if I had rested on my big but:

* But Cowboys don't sail yachts…
* But it cost too much money to buy a yacht…
* But what will people think…

- But what about pirates…
- But what about storms…

Resting on any one of the big buts would have ended my bodacious adventure before I even pursued it. Stop looking at your but, and start looking to your horizon and you will discover how you can make your bodacious dream a reality.

Be butless and be bodacious!

CHAPTER NINE

Know When You Are In the Barrel

ONE OF MY JOBS ON THE RANCH INVOLVED hauling cattle with a large tractor-trailer truck. I hauled cattle that had been purchased, cattle that were to be sold, or cattle that Arnold selected for slaughter. I recall that one day I left the ranch with a load of cattle to take the meatpacking operation. The ranch I worked on was unique in that Arnold, the owner, had his own custom meat packing operation. His goal was to raise the best cattle and provide the tenderest beef to his customers. By owning his own meat packing operation, Arnold controlled the quality from the pasture to the meat counter. Customers who bought meat from Arnold knew they would receive the best meat at fair prices.

After a two-hour drive with a full load of cattle, I arrived ahead of schedule at the meat packing operation and unloaded the nervous cattle into the holding pen. I am not sure how the cattle sensed it, but they were always very nervous when they were unloaded at the meat packing operation.

I was excited after I got the cattle unloaded. I had a date with Mattie that evening and hoped I would be able to take off a little early. Since the meat packing operation was under the same ownership as the ranch I could be recruited to help in the meat packing plant if they were short handed, and that is exactly what happened. Gary the manager of the slaughterhouse was taking a break and smoking a cigarette near the loading dock with a few of the other workers. As I passed by Gary, he grinned and said to the other workers, "I bet you that Cowboy will kill the pig."

He flipped out his long, razor sharp knife from the sheath attached to his belt, and handed me the knife. He said, "Cowboy, someone brought in a pig for us to slaughter. Would you go on the slaughter floor and cut the pig's throat? These old boys don't think you have it in you to kill that pig."

I was stunned by the challenge and really put on the spot. I did not want to kill the pig; I had never done anything like that before but knew if I refused the challenge, the other workers would kid me about being afraid. Instead of doing what I should have done and turned down the challenge, I took the knife and replied in a cocky manner to the whole group, "Don't know that I will need the knife, normally I kill pigs with my bare hands, but if it will make you boys feel better I will take the little knife."

Gary and the workers laughed as I turned and headed through the large sliding door that led to the slaughterhouse.

As the door slid closed behind me, I did not know what to expect. Was the pig going to be running loose on the killing floor? Was it a big pig or a little pig? All these were small details that I failed to ask about because of my cocky reply and self-confident attitude.

Not knowing what to expect, I held the butcher knife firmly in my grip just in case the pig lunged at me and I needed to protect myself.

Walking down the long poorly lit hall, the smell of the slaughter-house hung heavy in the air. I hated the slaughterhouse because of the smell and because it was darn right creepy. I did my best to avoid the slaughterhouse whenever I delivered cattle. However, today because I was too cocky, I had myself not only in the slaughterhouse, but I had a knife in my hand looking for a pig to cut his throat.

As I came nearer to the killing floor, I began asking myself, "What would be so bad about turning around and giving the knife back? Sure they would make fun of me, call me a little girl or worse, but it could not be worse than trying to kill a raging pig with this small knife."

The closer I came to the kill floor; in my mind, the pig became bigger and meaner. I feared a wild boar with long tusks, jumping from a hidden position and viciously attacking me. Maybe he would not kill me; instead, he would maim me, leaving me without a nose or ear. Perhaps this vicious pig might bite off a couple of my fingers or maybe even take an arm off.

By the time I rounded the corner and was in full view of the killing floor, I had worked myself into a tizzy thinking about the number of mad vicious pig attack scenarios. Good thing that Gary and the other workers did know what was going through my mind or the fear I felt, because they would have never let me forget it.

The adrenaline raced through my veins and my heart pounded in my chest as my eyes darted about the killing floor searching for the attacking pig. However, there was nothing there. There was no attacking pig; not even a sign that a pig had been there. So where was the pig? Then panic set back in as I thought, *The pig is hiding waiting to attack me.*

I stumbled wildly across the kill floor in an attempt to position myself to take on the pig. In my wild movements, I almost knocked over a large barrel that sat in the middle of the killing floor. It was as if the barrel came to life, it shook and rattled and wild squeals rang from the large steel barrel. I darted away from the barrel to a safe position and reasoned, *this pig must be more shrewd than I first thought; he's taken up a position in the barrel!*

This is one smart pig, I thought to myself as I moved slowly toward the violently shaking barrel. Slowly I moved forward as the barrel came to a rest. I figured the pig must have calmed down and repositioned for his death lunge to my face if I dared to look in the barrel. Slowly, I approached the barrel; my heart was pounding as I peeked over the edge and into the barrel. In a flash, I caught a glimpse of something black and heard a deep grunt just before a deafening squeal rang out from the barrel.

The hair stood on the back of my neck, and I moved to a defensive position just a short distance from the barrel. I gripped the butcher knife tightly as I prepared to defend myself against certain attack. The barrel shook wildly and danced around the killing floor as the pig thrashed about inside. After a wild period of activity, the pig settled down and was quiet inside the barrel. Now more than ever, I wanted to exit the kill floor, hand the knife back to Gary, and face my humiliation. However, my pride overwhelmed my sense of good judgment and once again, I advanced toward the barrel. This time there would be no retreat; this pig was going down!

Energized by adrenaline and motivated by my male pride, I boldly approached the barrel. Again, the barrel erupted into violent shaking when I peered over the side. To my surprise there was no wild boar with huge tusk, instead there was a small little black pig about the size of a poodle. I could not help but laugh at myself when I saw the little pig. In my mind I had created, a large vicious animal that was hell bent on taking me out. In reality, my large man-eating pig was nothing more than a small poodle dog-sized pig.

The little pig, exhausted from his attempts to escape the barrel, finally came to a rest in the bottom of the barrel. Small grunts came from the little pig as he struggled in his exhaustion for his next breath. His head hung low, and the little pig sat exhausted looking at the bottom of the barrel. The little pig slowly lifted his head, looked up from the bottom of the barrel, and got the first good look at his executioner.

Instead of being the wild vicious animal I had created in my mind, it was nothing more than a small exhausted pig imprisoned in a barrel. However, I had my assignment and had to move on to get the task accomplished. I positioned myself over the barrel then calculated how to take hold of the pig so I could cut his throat and end this quickly. As I bent over in the barrel to grasp hold of one of his ears, the little pig sprung to life and with renewed energy leaped high, and almost cleared the edge of the barrel. Startled by his surprise attack I fell backward onto the cold wet killing floor, pulling the barrel over as I fell. The metal barrel made a loud crashing sound as it hit the floor and rolled down the floor's slight incline.

I do not know how it all happened so quickly, but the little pig escaped from his barrel and was now loose on the kill floor running in a panic looking for an escape route. In my fall to the killing floor; I lost the butcher knife and was now unarmed to take on this little pig from hell. How did this happen? How did I go from executioner to an unarmed participant in this game of survival?

The little pig darted about the killing floor knocking over buckets, racks, and small barrels. The scene was deteriorating into a comic show and somehow I had become the star. Stumbling to my feet, I searched the floor for the butcher knife so I could somehow finish the job.

With all the commotion, coming from the kill floor it was only a matter of time before Gary came to see what was going on. I knew I had only moments to do in the pig in and save my reputation. To my relief I found the butcher knife near a drain in the center of the floor. I grabbed the knife tightly and turned to locate the pig. In a flash, the little pig darted across the floor and ran into the slaughter chute where the cattle met their final demise. The little pig made a big mistake by running into the chute, because he was trapped with only one way out and that was by me. I followed the little pig into the chute and saw him standing in the far corner, heaving heavily for each breath. I approached the exhausted little pig that was trapped in the corner with no place to go with full intent of finishing the task.

Then I had to face reality, I could not kill the pig. I never wanted to kill the pig and had without success attempted to convince myself that I could do the deed. I paused for a moment to catch my breath and that little pig seized the opportunity and made a determined dash between my legs. I did not try to catch him, nor did I attempt to harm him with the knife, I just did not have it in me to kill the pig, so I watched him run out of the chute to his relative freedom.

I heard Gary's raging voice behind me, "What in the heck happened here? I asked you to do a simple job and instead you wrecked my killing floor." The other workers broke out in a roar of laughter as Gary commenced to give me a good chewing out as the little pig darted about the room.

"Give me the knife; I should not have sent a little girl to do a man's job," Gary said as he extended his hand for the knife.

I turned the knife over to Gary, walked past the taunting workers, and made my way out the back door and toward my truck. Never in my life had I felt so embarrassed by failure. Instead of facing more ridicule, I started the cattle truck and left.

BODACIOUS CHALLENGES REQUIRE BODACIOUS PERSISTENCE

I have often thought about my encounter with the little pig. Logistically the little pig was at a disadvantage trapped in the barrel with no means of protection. Even with this huge disadvantage, the little pig won. He beat me. How did this happen? I was better equipped with my butcher knife; I was larger and supposedly smarter than the little pig. But the little pig won not because he was better equipped, in a more favorable environment or even because he was smarter. The little pig won because he knew he was in the barrel and harnessed extraordinary persistence, unrestrained passion, and the determination to take bold action and win.

Extraordinary persistence and the unrestrained passion to win are most often the determining factors in success. Extraordinary persistence and unrestrained passion will win out over the best equipped, the largest, or the most favorable environment. The little pig was "in the barrel." It is not unusual for us to find ourselves "in the barrel" from time to time. Remember, just because you are in the most favorable position to win doesn't' mean you will prevail. It is when you are "in the barrel, facing bodacious challenges," that extraordinary persistence and unrestrained passion to win will make the difference.

PERSIST IN SURVIVAL

The little pig in the barrel demonstrated an unrestrained passion for survival and extraordinary persistence in his effort to live. Trapped and exhausted in the bottom of the barrel, the little pig fought for survival. The little pig knew he was in the bottom of the barrel, and if he wanted to live then he would have to take bold action. His unrestrained passion for survival and extraordinary persistence allowed him to escape

You will encounter times when you are in the bottom of the barrel, so you must be able to assess your position accurately. The first step is to come clean with yourself and realize that you really are in the bottom of the barrel.

When you are in the bottom of the barrel, you must have the unrestrained passion to survive and extraordinary persistence not to give up. Just as the exhausted little pig, found one last bit of energy to jump high from the bottom of the barrel and set things in motion for his escape, so you must take bold action, grasp your last bit of energy, and leap high during your most challenging times. You have heard it said, "It is darkest before the dawn," so when it seems to be your darkest hour, reach for your last bit of inspiration and energy and jump from the bottom of your barrel.

PERSIST IN RELATIONSHIPS

You may find you are at the bottom of the barrel with important relationships. Exhausted from your efforts to heal hurt relationships, you will be tempted to give up and let the relationship die. You may feel you have done all you can do in the relationship; and that it is time for the other person to respond. This is when you have to reach a little deeper and go beyond yourself and your exhaustion to jump higher. Use the last bit of your relationship energy to escape from the bottom of the relationship barrel.

Surviving relationships that are in the bottom of the barrel can be the most challenging and exhausting because of the amount of emotion involved. When the relationship is close and the emotion is high then great effort is required for the relationship to survive.

Thankfully, Mattie has been there to encourage and even admonish me when I was at the bottom of various relationship barrels. She has and continues to press me forward, motivate me, and inspire me. She has had the courage to tell me, "Get up, stop your whining, be persistent, be passionate, you have not tried hard enough. This relationship is too important for you to lie there in defeat."

You need someone like Mattie who has the courage to look over the edge of your barrel to push you to jump higher and to persist in an extraordinary way. Find the person who is best able to give you encouragement, then drop your pride and put aside your emotion and listen to them.. Healing your most damaged and important relationships will require extraordinary persistence, unrestrained passion, and bold action.

PERSIST IN PERSONAL CHALLENGES

One Monday morning I was driving an empty cattle truck back to the ranch to pick up another load of cattle. Mondays were the only days I returned with an empty truck. All other days I would stop by the local cattle auction barn and return with a load that Arnold had purchased the day before. Good thing the truck was empty that day because about half way to the ranch the truck started sputtering and blowing black smoke. I pulled onto the side of the road and drove slowly hoping I would make it to the next small town where maybe I could find a repair shop. I limped the truck into the town of Riverview where I noticed a sign that read "Buddy's Repair Shop." I slowly pulled into the driveway of the repair shop as the truck spewed a black cloud from the tail pipe and died. I was relieved that had I made it to the repair shop and even more relieved I did not have a load of cattle banging around in the back.

I stepped from the truck and walked across the gravel driveway toward the office. Behind a fence next to the repair shop, a large black dog drooled and barked wildly as he strained the chain that prevented him from jumping the fence and taking a chunk out of my butt. The office door flew open and an older man with a cane in his hand and wearing a dirty ball cap shouted, "Shut up that barking Harley! Sorry, about Harley, he is a lot more bark than bite; but he sure can be annoying. What can I do for you?"

"Well my truck started missing, spewing black smoke and it died right after I pulled in your driveway. Can you look at it?" I asked. The old man tapped the ground with his cane and moved slowly toward my truck. As I watched the old man negotiate his way toward my

137

truck, I realized he was blind. After a lot of tapping the ground and shuffling about, he located my truck and began running his hands over the front of the truck and feeling his way around the bumpers and then along the side. After his examination of the truck he stated with confidence, "This is a 1968 Loadmaster, so you are in luck; I have worked on a lot of them. Let me get one of the boys to help us get it inside so we can look at it."

Amazed that the old man identified the truck by running his hands over it I asked him, "Sir, how did you know the make and year of this truck by just running your hands over it?"

The old man shuffled toward me and said, "Son I was not always blind, and before I lost my eyesight I worked as a mechanic, so I have worked on a lot of these old trucks. When I went blind, I made my mind up that I was not going to sit back and do nothing. I love to fix cars; and I decided that I was not going to let being blind keep me from doing what I love to do. It took me a while to figure out how to do it, but I learned to see with my hands. When I put my hands on a truck or the engine, vivid images of what I once could see come to mind and it's like I can see again."

Once the truck was inside the repair shop, the old man climbed on a stool, leaned over the fender under the open hood and started feeling his way around the engine. On command, his helper would hand the old man his tools and reposition the stool as needed. It was amazing to watch the old man remove parts and feel his way around the engine.

"Looks like you have fouled injectors, give us about an hour and we will have you back on the road." The old man said as he climbed from the stool.

After working with his helper for about an hour, the old man climbed into the cab of the truck, turned the ignition key and the diesel engine started with a roar. He sat behind the wheel of the truck and revved the engine. Then the old man said to me, "Climb in and I will take you for a ride around the block for a little test drive." After a brief pause he continued, "You are not afraid to ride with a blind man are you?"

Of course, I was afraid to ride with a blind man! His request caught me off guard and at a loss for words, so I replied fumbling for words, "Well, I am kind of in a hurry, and it sounds like the engine is running good so I trust you that everything is okay." The old man gave the engine a big rev, threw his head back with a roaring laugh and he replied, "At least I know you're not stupid enough to ride with a blind man! I was kidding you boy, the truck is running great now."

The old man had a passion for fixing cars and did not let his personal challenge of blindness stand in the way of pursuing his passion. For good reason he could have quit and given into his personal challenge, but he exercised extraordinary persistence to overcome his personal challenge and adapted so he could pursue his passion. The old man understood that he "was in the barrel," so he properly assessed his position and took action so he could continue working on cars. The old man did not live in denial about his condition, nor did he let his anger or self-pity overcome his desire to pursue his passion.

Most everyone has some type of personal challenge to overcome. Your challenge may be physical, it may be financial, inadequate education, or you have experienced abuse, discrimination, or traumatic life events. No matter your personal challenge, you cannot allow it to keep you in the "bottom of the barrel". Learn a lesson from Buddy the blind mechanic and do not let your personal challenges prevent you from pursuing your passion. Bodacious challenges require extraordinary persistence, unrestrained passion, and bold action to overcome. Take the leap, pursue your passion and persist to overcome.

PERSIST IN YOUR PASSIONS

The little pig had a passion for survival, while the odds were against him; the little pig was unrestrained in his desire to get out of the barrel. Life is about more than just living in the survival mode and having passion for survival. Always living life in the survival mode will wear you down and prevent you from pursuing your passions. Instead, live your life persisting in pursuit of your passions. You will find when you pursue what you are passionate about you will spend less time in the barrel and less time in survival mode.

As you pursue your passion you will face doubters and critics. However, extraordinary persistence and unrestrained pursuit of your passion will keep you on the course. It is interesting that often your biggest critics will be the skeptical people who failed to pursue their own passions and want to keep everyone else at their level of mediocrity. Be extraordinarily persistent in pursuit of your passions because persistence during times of discouragement makes all the difference.

Be unrestrained in your beliefs and then live and persist in your beliefs. I am passionate and unrestrained in my beliefs and remain bold in my convictions when I face doubters and critics. My beliefs define me, refine me, direct me, and fuel my passion for living. Embrace your beliefs and be passionate about your beliefs. By doing this you will discover your purpose in life. Live your life in alignment with your passions and purpose, and you will discover the real joy of living.

PERSIST IN LEARNING

When I worked for Charlie, I not only learned about giving, but he also taught me the value of continued learning. I remember going in his office each week to get my paycheck; his office looked as much like a library as it did an office. Huge bookcases stuffed with books lined the walls floor to ceiling. During one of my visits, I asked Charlie why he had so many books. He simply said, "I read so that I am not ignorant. You can go through life knowing about things, or you can be ignorant. These books can educate you on about anything you need to know. If you want to know something, someone probably has written a book on it."

Then Charlie posed a question, "Do you want to be ignorant?" There was really only one response:, "No sir, I do not want to be ignorant."

Charlie went back to writing my paycheck and then looked me straight in the eye and said, "This isn't much of a paycheck. It is a shame you worked so hard this week and made so little. You can change how much is on your paycheck if you are committed to not being ignorant. Continued learning and the willingness to work hard are the keys to writing yourself a bigger paycheck. You have the hard work part down, but you are not doing too well on the learning part. It is up to you, work hard for little or work hard and smart for a lot. Do not be ignorant, balance what you are learning in three areas and you can change your life:

* Spiritual

* Occupational

* Personal

Charlie picked up an old tattered Bible from the corner of his desk, "First and foremost, spend time in spiritual study every day. I start my day reading the Bible, but I do not stop there; I also read books about my Christian faith and gain a deeper understanding of my faith. My spiritual study time is the most valuable and most relaxing time of the day."

Charlie then stood up and walked over to the big window in his office, "Please, come over here and look out the window. What do you see?"

From the vantage point of his office that sat atop the highest hill on the ranch, you could see for several miles, "Well sir, I see a lot of cattle and some really good farm land."

Charlie continued, "It was not always like that. When I first bought this land, it was covered with cactus and mesquite trees. It took a lot of hard work to clear the land and get it in condition to plow and plant. Beyond the hard work, it required a lot of learning. When I was building this ranch into what you see today, I studied daily about cattle ranching and farming. These bookcases are full of books about ranching and farming. The knowledge I got from these books has been invaluable and taught me how to create a successful farming and ranching operation. By studying what was in these books, I was able to write myself a bigger paycheck. So study everything you can about your occupation, and you can write yourself a bigger paycheck."

Charlie sat back in his office chair and said, "Do you know the nice thing about having a bigger paycheck? You get to have fun and do things you enjoy doing outside of your work. For me, I love to go places and see different things and the way people live in other parts of the world. Many of the books on these shelves are about travel destinations. Reading allows me to travel around the world without ever leaving the comfort of my chair. When I do decide to go somewhere, I have read about where I am going and know what to see, where to stay, and about the local customs. I enjoy reading about other places in the world and planning my trips. Travel is what I like to do when I am not working, and I encourage you to find something you enjoy doing besides working. Reading about my personal interests is relaxing and allows me to escape the stresses of life. Therefore, I encourage you to read about something that you enjoy doing. Learn about your personal interests and you will enjoy doing them even more."

Charlie reached across his desk, handed me my paycheck, and said with a smile, "You really deserve more than just a paycheck, so read about your spiritual life, your occupation and your personal interests and you will realize your dreams. The sad thing is most people stop learning when they get out of school; they figure they have their education so there is no need to study. Instead of reading, they choose to sit in front of the television night after night polluting their mind with meaningless junk. Be persistent and have a passion for continuing your learning and you will not be ignorant, you will be happy. Build a big bookcase, and you will build a big paycheck and a big life."

Charlie passed away a few years ago; however, his teachings continue to live on and have made a profound difference in my life. Charlie taught me how to earn more, become more, care more and give more. He embodied extraordinary persistence and unrestrained passion and boldly inspired a young cowboy not to be ignorant. Choose not to be ignorant; choose to be extraordinary, unrestrained, and bold in your continued learning.

PERSIST BODACIOUSLY WITHOUT FEAR

Your biggest enemy of persistence and pursuing your passion is fear. Be careful that you do not create your own "vicious wild boar with long tusk" when your challenge is only a "little pig." I defeated myself before I ever found the little pig in the barrel, because in my mind I had created a terribly vicious opponent that was going to eat me alive.

Unsubstantiated fear will prevent you from effectively taking on the bodacious challenges that you will face. While having reasonable caution based on facts is prudent, be careful not to create your own monster based on unfounded opinions or fears.

When I was a young man, I feared public speaking and had no knowledge of how to deliver a message to a group. My job requirements had expanded and required that I speak in front of groups. Getting in front of people to speak was my "vicious wild boar." I realized I had to overcome this fear and gain competency in this area so I enrolled in a public speaking course and began speaking weekly by leading a small group at my local church. At first public speaking was uncomfortable and was at times terrifying, but over time and after speaking in front of groups, I found my fear was unfounded and really no more than a "little pig".

Today, I speak comfortably in front of groups of all sizes; it does not matter if I am speaking in front of ten people or a thousand people. What was once a great fear is now one of my strengths. Take your fears on and do not let "little pigs" become your "viscous wild boars."

Pursue your passions, persist in your challenges, overcome your fears, and then you can leap from the bottom of your barrel and realize your bodacious dreams.

- Know when you are in the barrel
- Be Bodacious in your persistence
- Persist to survive
- Persist to grow
- Persist in relationships
- Persist in challenges
- Persist in your passions
- Persist without fear

IMPORTANT INSTRUCTIONS
FOR THE READER

You have finished reading the journal and the Bodacious Secrets. Your next step is to return this journal and cowboy picture for additional instructions.

The Bodacious Secrets Passed On

CHAPTER TEN

Bodacious Leadership Revealed

OPENING A DRAWER ON THE SIDE OF HIS DESK, Josh removed an overstuffed brown envelop with CON-FIDENTIAL written boldly across the front. He stood up, handed me the envelope, and instructed, "Go ahead, open the envelope and look inside. What is inside this envelope will explain the Bodacious Secrets. I apologize for the ragged condition of the journal and the picture of the cowboys; both of them have a few miles on them. It was years ago that I sat across the desk from Cowboy when he handed me this same envelope."

Josh then walked over to the picture of the five cowboys hanging on the wall and said, "Luke, when Cowboy gave me the journal I promised to read it every day and return it to him when I finished it. Today reminds me of the day I returned the journal to Cowboy; I had a similar meeting with him just as we are having today. During my meeting with Cowboy, he instructed me to live by the Bodacious

Secrets and pass them on. On that day, I promised Cowboy that I would pass the journal on to another young man who would promise to do the same."

LUKE'S STORY

I can verify that Josh lived up to his promise to Cowboy because he found me when I was a struggling young man, and passed the journal on to me. Just as Josh did when he returned the journal to Cowboy, I returned the journal and promised to "pass it on."

A few years have passed now, and I can state that the journal and the Bodacious Secrets have made a profound impact on my life. After working under Josh's guidance for a while, he recommended me to one of his friends who owned a manufacturing operation in a nearby city. I am grateful for Josh's help because the opportunity at the new company has been great for me. Even though I do not occupy the corner office yet, I do have a high-level job running the sales organization.

Just as Josh mentored me to do, I walk through the factory and across the loading dock every morning in search of the next recipient to fulfill my promise and pass it on.

As I was making my rounds across the loading dock, a voice called from behind me, "Looking for someone to share a bodacious secret with?"

Surprised by the statement, I turned to find Josh standing near one of the loading dock doors. It had been a while since I last spoke with Josh and even longer since he visited me where I worked.

"Josh, what brings you here? Are you out loafing today?" I asked while extending my hand to his.

"Well I think the operation will do fine without me this morning. Luke, I need to talk to you in private, do you mind if we go somewhere to talk?" Josh asked.

Detecting seriousness in his tone, I replied, "Sure we can go up to my office, it's not as nice as yours, but we can visit there."

As we walked through the factory a number of people greeted me with, "Good morning, Luke."

Josh commented as we walked toward the office, "Looks like you are keeping the tradition alive, seems like everyone knows you."

We arrived at my office and Josh and I got a cup of coffee and sat down to talk. Josh stirred his coffee and looked around the office, "Looks like you have done well for yourself. I'm glad this worked out for you. Sorry, I have not been by lately, but things have been pretty busy over at the office."

"Josh, it's just good to see you again. It seems like things get too busy at times, so tell me what brings you here today. You seemed a little serious in your tone downstairs."

"Luke, before I get to the point, let me give you a little background. Over the years, I have had the opportunity to meet with Cowboy often to receive coaching on the Bodacious Secrets. After Cowboy retired and left me in charge of the company, he and Mattie spent time with their grandchildren and enjoyed sailing in the Caribbean. We spoke often by phone to discuss the business and met when he was in town between his sailing trips.

It was an honor when Cowboy and Mattie invited Sarah and me to sail with him and Mattie in the Virgin Islands. For ten days, we sailed from island to island, enjoyed sugar white beaches and evening skies full of stars. This was the most memorable trip of my life, and I learned so much from Cowboy during this time.

Cowboy never really retired; he just turned the page to another bodacious chapter of his life. When he was not with the grandchildren or sailing, he kept his calendar booked with speaking engagements. Cowboy became a well-known speaker and spoke often to sales organizations and leadership groups, I know you have attended some of his talks and even had the opportunity to spend some time with him. He was excited to know you were the recipient of his journal and asked me often about how you were doing."

Josh paused and appeared visibly shaken as he stirred in his chair. Struggling to speak the next words, he continued, "Cowboy did a lot for me; he was a mentor and close friend. Yesterday, Cowboy passed away. His funeral is tomorrow, and Mattie wanted me to ask if you would be a pallbearer, because Cowboy spoke of you often as a recipient of his journal."

Without hesitation I replied, "He did a lot for me as well, and I am sorry to hear about his passing. Of course I will be a pallbearer."

Josh nodded his head as a tear ran down his cheek. He continued, "Thankfully, I did get a chance to visit with him prior to his passing. Cowboy requested that I publish his journal and reveal the Bodacious Secrets to more people. To be honest with you Luke, I am not much of a writer and I need some help. Therefore, I want to pass this bodacious opportunity on to you. If you will write the book, I will help you with the stories and see that it is published. How about it Luke, will you write the book?"

Evident by the book you are now reading, I agreed to write the book. Josh and I worked for months on this book and it is our honor to share Cowboy's journal and the Bodacious Secrets with you.

Just as Cowboy and Josh did, every day I walk from the office, to the factory floor and the loading dock looking for the next recipient of the journal. By writing this book, I pursued a bodacious opportunity, and now I share Cowboy's journal with anyone who will read it. Through the pages of this book, the Bodacious Secrets are passed to you. The challenge to you is to Be Bodacious and Put Life in Your Leadership.

Be Bodacious and pass the secrets to the next "Cowboy!"